Around the WORLD in three terms

All the Recipes You Need to Sail Through the School Year,
by the Well-travelled Families and Friends
of a Wimbledon School

BG Books

First published in the United Kingdom in 2014 by BG Books
Bishop Gilpin Church of England Primary School
Lake Road, London SW19 7LN

ISBN 978-0-9565523-7-2

publishing team:

Editor: Mel Barrett
Design: Basia Pacześna-Vercueil
Design Support: Alessandra Ferrrari Ellis
Recipe Editor/Interviews: Mel Barrett
Photography: Families from Bishop Gilpin
and Deborah Albert, Mel Barrett, Kitty Gallanaugh,
Tom Hopkinson, Sampson Lloyd,
Francesca McKenna, Basia Pacześna-Vercueil
Illustrations: Children from Bishop Gilpin
and Basia Pacześna-Vercueil
Editorial Support: Tristan Hopkinson, **Ruth** Mair Howard-Jones, Sally
Le Marquand
Photo shoot styling: Mel Barrett, Ruth Mair Howard-Jones
Proofreaders: Susannah Hamilton, Kate Oppenheim,
Katie Preston, Vicky Williams-Ellis

Printed and bound in Poland

Contents

Introduction 4
Travel Tips 6

the autumn/winter term 8

'Back to School' Breakfasts 10
Autumn Picnic 16
Apple Day 22
Autumn Feasts and Festivals 26
Christmas 54

the spring term 68

Cheap and Healthy Meals 70
Winter Soul Food 76
The School Cake Sale 86
Spring High Days and Holidays 92
Easter 106

the summer term 114

Quick and Easy Meals 116
Brain Food 126
Post-match Refreshments 130
Lunch Boxes and Picnics 136
Summer Parties 144

Thank yous 156
Index 158

Introduction

The cooking challenges faced by most busy families are not unique:
at certain times of the year – Christmas, for example – we have crowds
to feed. In winter we gravitate towards warming dishes that will sustain
us through the long, dark days; later in the year we want food that can be
threaded on to skewers or packed up and eaten al fresco. And there are
plenty of moments, such as the dreaded school cake sale, when we need
to grapple with a cake tin and an electric whisk. Fed up with the late-night
trawl for the right recipe for the right moment, it occurred to us that, with
the collective know-how of over 300 families at our fingertips, we could
pool our expertise. This book is the result.

Being a London school – our families come from over 35 different
countries; 27% of our pupils do not have English as their first language
– we were privileged to be able to cast our net around the world for
inspiration. So, for example, our families from some of the world's great
rice cultures share the secrets of fragrant curries and stews, perfect for
large gatherings; our families from warmer climes inspire us with recipes
for just the sort of food – Catalan paella, for example – that we want to be
eating in the sunshine; and, our Japanese mums show us how to make
the ultimate packed lunch for fussy eaters.

Many of the recipes in this book are authentic representations
of the cuisine of far-away regions and distant lands, handed down through
the generations and never written down before, let alone published.
Some are old faithfuls from much-loved cookbooks. All, however, have
one thing in common: they are tried and tested favourites that have always
managed to hit the spot for our families. We hope that they help you too,
as you journey through the school year!

BY SOPHIA

Headteacher's foreword

Sun-kissed holidays and treasured memories are only ever an evocative taste or aroma away. We hope that this book will inspire your families to prepare and cook new dishes together, enjoy new tastes and create new memories to last a lifetime.

Our richly diverse community has infused this book with flavours from around the world. The recipes in this book tell tales of families enjoying good food; and good food, like good stories, should be shared. So I am very grateful to the editors for their passion, skill and commitment in creating such a wonderful book of recipes for us all to enjoy.

Matt Ball

Notes on recipes

Although we have rigorously checked every recipe, and indeed cooked a great many of them for our photo shoots, we can't claim to have tested each one for the purposes of this book. Moreover, we've had to do a fair bit of tinkering, particularly where units of measurement were unfamiliar to British readers (decilitres, for example), quantities less than precise and language unclear.

Just in case something has been lost in translation, may we suggest, as many cookbooks have done before us, that you use the recipe as a guideline only. No recipe is foolproof – it is impossible for the writer to account for the variations in each reader's kitchen (fresh ingredients such as eggs and lemons do not roll off a production line in standard weights; ovens have hotter spots and other peculiarities; different types of pan conduct heat at different rates). Much better to use your senses, rather than slavishly adhering to somebody else's words: cut into meat and reheated foods, and feel whether they are piping hot in the middle; test vegetables and rice by eating a piece (and adjust cooking times accordingly); cover dishes loosely with foil if the outer surface is browning too fast whilst the inside still needs more time in the oven; check bubbling pots to make sure they are not boiling dry (and top up with liquid if need be).

Except when it comes to baking, it's usually the case that exact measurements don't matter. Real cooking is about taking a recipe and making it your own: a bit more spice here; a bit less sugar there; a switch to lower-fat milk or cream cheese; butter instead of oil; oil instead of butter. Before the days of corporate teams of home economists and stylists, this was the way people cooked.

So please take these recipes, try them, change them, make them your own, and, most importantly, don't forget to pass them on!

NB Recipes have been submitted from a range of individuals from our school community, including pupils, parents, staff members and even a few grandparents. We have referenced current pupils only (not siblings) in the recipes from our families.

Travel tips

You may find on these pages, as you travel through the year, one or two ingredients that you have never come across before. Do not be daunted! With a little thought and imagination you will be able to travel the world easily. Here are a few tips to help you on your way:

Visit new neighbourhoods.
In our neck of the woods we're just a short 219 or 493 bus-ride away from Tooting Broadway, where you can find tubs of pureed ginger and garlic, enormous bunches of fresh herbs such as fenugreek, and all sorts of useful items in the freezer counter, for example sliced okra. Or take the train a few stops to New Malden, where you can shop for Pokemon-shaped nori seaweed (see page 136) and tasty Korean marinades (page 152).

Seek out insider knowledge.
Ask any Polish friend and they will know exactly where to go for the best smoked sausages or good soft cheese (and it won't be the local supermarket!). Friends, neighbours and colleagues from overseas are a mine of information, and will almost certainly be delighted to share their sources with you. (Thanks to Wajeeha for showing us her favourite store in Tooting, Winny for pointing out where to find Asian pears, and Juwon for treating us to bulgogi in a fantastic restaurant on Burlington Road, New Malden!)

Make friends with your local suppliers.
They are a fantastic resource, and are often very happy to take special requests.

Explore the 'World Foods' section of your local supermarket.
Salt cod, sushi rice and wasabi paste are just a few of the products now available on many a high street.

Don't be afraid to adapt recipes
with more easily available substitutes. Although in this book you'll find plenty of interesting ways of using up seasonal British stalwarts such as apples (page 22), strawberries (page 135), beetroot (page 78), and cabbage (page 73), why not try applying the flavours found on these pages to different ingredients: pears dipped in chocolate taste just as good as more exotic specimens! (page 125)

WHY NOT TRY ASKING ME FOR ANY SPECIAL REQUIREMENTS — YOU'LL BE SURPRISED WHAT I CAN SOURCE FOR YOU, FOR EXAMPLE HUMANELY-REARED ROSE VEAL (SEE PAGE 27), SPECIAL SCOTTISH LORNE SAUSAGES (PAGE 82) AND PAPER-THIN SIRLOIN (PAGE 152)

This is Martin, our local butcher.

YOU'LL OFTEN SEE ME DRIVING AROUND THE NEIGHBOURHOOD, DELIVERING MY BOXES OF ORGANIC FRUIT AND VEG. SEASONAL BRITISH PRODUCE IS USUALLY MUCH CHEAPER THAN IMPORTED VEG AND WORKS BEAUTIFULLY IN MANY OF THESE RECIPES.

Tooting Broadway

This is Simon, the veg man

(and BG dad!)

I CAN GET YOU GOOD VALUE OLIVE OIL AND LEMONS FULL OF FLAVOUR

Korean shop

This is Mimmo, from the Italian deli

down the road

the Autumn/ Winter term

CHAPTER ONE

Sheets of name labels plop through the letter box; crisp shirts lie waiting in plastic packets; the last few stubborn grains of summer sand have finally been swept away. It's the start of a new school year, when – for a few days at least – our children will be packed off to school with polished shoes, perfectly ironed clothes and a nutritious breakfast inside them. In this chapter we bring you some favourite breakfast recipes to help get the term off to a good start, along with some ideas to help make the most of the autumn sunshine, before the clocks go back and the nights start to draw in. Plus we have some great recipes to see you through the feasts and festivals of the season, and to fill your house with the sweet, spicy smell of Christmas.

'back to school'
Breakfasts

Start the term as you mean to go on...
Here are some of our favourite breakfasts

Apple Muesli

Lisa (mum to Amber Newsom Davis)

SERVES 3

My Grandma Edwards (Moma) used to make this for me when I was a child, and now my children love it too.
Grate two apples (Granny Smiths are best for this) and add to a mixing bowl with 100g oats, a generous handful
of dried cranberries and a generous squeeze of fresh lemon juice. Give it all a good stir and serve in bowls.
We love this with a drizzle of condensed milk on the top.

Wholemeal Mini Pancakes

The Gratrick Family (Tilly)

MAKES 20-30 MINI PANCAKES

These are a firm favourite with our family and also a great way of getting kids to eat lots of fresh fruit! Mix 250g
self-raising wholemeal flour with 25g sugar, a pinch of baking powder and a pinch of sea salt. Whisk 2 medium
eggs and add to the mix. Add 275ml milk and 50g melted butter and mix well. Place a teaspoon or two
of sunflower oil in a frying pan (to stop the pancakes from sticking), then drop spoonfuls of batter into the pan
(pancakes should be about 4cm in diameter). Once you see little bubbles appear flip the pancake over. Repeat
until all the batter is gone. Serve warm with various fruits, bacon, jams, chocolate spread, butter, etc. You can
adapt the recipe by adding different items to the mixture like sultanas, blueberries, orange zest or maple syrup.

Eggy Bread

Freddie Sherratt

SERVES 1

I love cooking eggy bread because it's really quick and easy to do. I cook it by myself for breakfast at weekends,
and sometimes before school if I get up early enough. Here's how you make it: crack one egg in a bowl and beat
with a whisk. Place a thick slice of bread in the eggy mixture and let the egg soak into it. Turn the bread over and
do the same for the other side. Heat a knob of butter in a frying pan until it is bubbling then slip in the bread
and fry on one side for approximately 2 minutes until golden-brown. Turn over and fry the other side for another
2 minutes until golden-brown. Eat immediately!

Apple and Cinnamon Porridge

The Blair Family (Robin)

SERVES 2 SMALL PEOPLE OR 1 HUNGRY ONE!

As the weather gets more autumnal, here's an addictive and very easy porridge recipe to begin the day.
Measure one small cup each of jumbo porridge oats, water and milk into a large Pyrex bowl. The cups shouldn't
be full — as if you were making tea or coffee. Peel a small apple. When the peel is removed, use the peeler
to shave the rest of the apple into the same bowl in wafer-thin slices. Stir to mix. Microwave on medium power
for about 7 or 8 minutes, stirring once or twice, until the porridge is thick and creamy. Add a dusting of sugar
and cinnamon to taste. Or place all ingredients in a saucepan and bring to the boil gently, stirring occasionally.
Then simmer on a low to medium heat for about 5 or 6 minutes, stirring frequently, until the porridge is thick
and creamy. Leave to stand for a minute (it will thicken slightly) before adding sugar and cinnamon.

Canadian Pancakes

Tim (dad to Hannah Evans)

MAKES 8

I spent three years in Edmonton, Canada and loved their pancakes — particularly when it was minus 30°C! Now I make them for special Sunday brunches. Serve them with bacon and maple syrup, sausages and maple syrup (Piggies in a Blanket as one family restaurant called them) or alternatively with yoghurt, fruit (delicious with blueberries and raspberries) and as always, maple syrup.

190G FLOUR (SUGGEST MIXING PLAIN AND STRONG BREAD FLOUR IF YOU HAVE IT. OTHERWISE USE PLAIN FLOUR)

2 TABLESPOONS GRANULATED SUGAR

2 TEASPOONS BAKING POWDER

1/2 TEASPOON SALT

1 EGG. BEATEN

1 CUP MILK

1 TABLESPOON COOKING OIL

Preheat the oven to 50°C/125°F. Mix the dry ingredients together then add the egg, milk and oil and stir. Don't worry too much about lumps; it's better not to over-mix. Heat the flattest pan you have on a medium heat, smeared with a little oil to avoid sticking. When the pan is hot enough (a drop of mixture should start to turn golden-brown) pour a ladle's worth of mixture into the pan. Start with one pancake, even if you have room for more, until you get the settings right (the first pancake is often an experiment!). The key is that it should spread slowly out to a diameter of about 10cm. If the mixture moves too quickly, it is too thin – just add a bit more flour to the mixture. Likewise, try adding more milk if the mixture seems too stiff. Wait until you see bubbles appearing across most of the surface and the bottom is golden-brown. (If the bottom is beginning to burn before the bubbles are appearing, turn down the heat a bit. Likewise, if it's all too slow, turn up the heat a little). Flip the pancake over and cook until both sides are golden-brown, then keep warm in the preheated oven.

"32% OF SCHOOLCHILDREN REGULARLY MISS BREAKFAST. A HUNGRY CHILD IS MORE LIKELY TO BE RESTLESS, UNHAPPY, LETHARGIC, DISTRACTED OR DISRUPTIVE IN LESSONS."

Source: registered charity Magic Breakfast (www.magicbreakfast.com)

Nicholas' Breakfast Smoothie

Nicholas Hogarth

SERVES 2

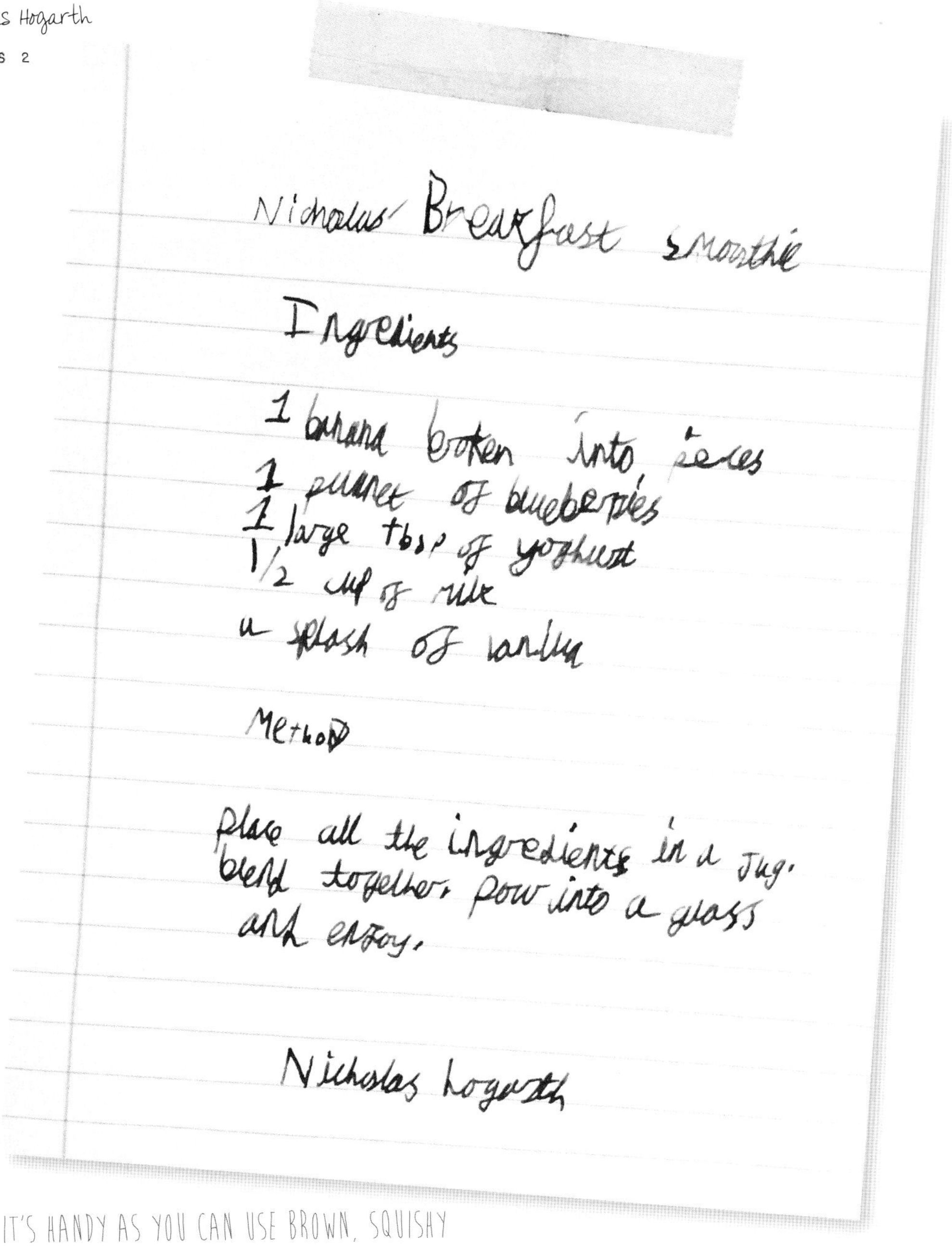

Nicholas' Breakfast smoothie

Ingredients

1 banana broken into pieces
1 punnet of blueberries
1 large tbsp of yoghurt
1/2 cup of milk
a splash of vanilla

Method

Place all the ingredients in a jug.
blend together, pour into a glass
and enjoy.

Nicholas Hogarth

"IT'S HANDY AS YOU CAN USE BROWN, SQUISHY
BANANAS AND FROZEN BLUEBERRIES. THEN YOU'VE
SENT THEM OFF TO SCHOOL WITH 2 OUT OF 5 A DAY
ALREADY TICKED OFF!"

Liz Ledaca (Nicholas' mum)

South African Rusks

Basia (mum to Sofia, Ania and Derik Vercueil)

MAKES APPROXIMATELY 35-40

Whenever we visit my husband's family back in South Africa, it is a tradition to wake up in the morning to a cup of coffee from my father-in-law (the barista!) and a couple of rusks on the side. Rusks are little light, dry, twice-baked breads or cakes, similar to Italian biscotti. These little chunks of joy are very popular in South Africa for breakfast (they feel indulgent yet are packed full of goodness), or as a healthy mid-afternoon snack (my children often have them after school). This recipe, given to me by my sister-in-law, Erica, is a favourite breakfast in our household. Delicious dunked into a cup of coffee!

225G BUTTER
2 SMALL EGGS
425G SELF-RAISING FLOUR
150G BRAN FLAKES
75G OAT BRAN
100G CASTER SUGAR
1 TEASPOON CINNAMON
1/2 TEASPOON SALT
1/4 CUP DESSICATED
  COCONUT (OPTIONAL)
1/2 CUP OF DRIED FRUIT
  AND SEEDS, EG
  CRANBERRIES, SUNFLOWER
  AND PUMPKIN SEEDS
  (OPTIONAL)
300ML BUTTERMILK

First bake: Preheat the oven to 180°C/350°F/Gas Mark 4. Grease 2 x 20cm rectangular loaf tins. Melt the butter in a small pan over a low heat. Whisk the eggs in a separate bowl until fluffy and opaque. Place the dry ingredients in a large bowl and mix together. Make a well in the middle, then pour in the melted butter, whisked eggs and buttermilk, and stir together using a wooden spoon. The mixture will be quite thick, so you can also use your hands to combine the ingredients, as you would with bread dough. Once you have a well-mixed dough, transfer half of the mix into each baking tin. Bake in the oven for 45-60 minutes until golden-brown on top, and a knife inserted into the centre comes out clean. Remove from the oven and leave to cool in the tins.

Second bake: Preheat the oven to 100°C/200°F. Remove the cooled loaves from the tins and cut each one into slices approximately 5cm thick, then cut each slice into 4 pieces. Place the rusks on a baking sheet and bake for approximately 6 hours (or overnight) until completely dried out. Store in an airtight container.

Alexander's English Breakfast Salad

The Bradley Family (Alexander)

SERVES 3

A simple recipe which we love to do for Sunday brunch. Many years ago we came across a similar salad in a café in France, and since then we have played around with the recipe, trying to recreate the original. We never quite succeeded, but no matter – it still tastes delicious. This simple version we call an English Breakfast salad (not sure the French café would approve!).

100G SMOKED BACON, CHOPPED
3 TOMATOES, CHOPPED INTO QUARTERS
100G ROCKET LEAVES
A SPLASH OF BALSAMIC VINEGAR
A DRIZZLE OF OLIVE OIL
3 EGGS

Put rocket leaves and tomatoes in a large bowl, add the oil and vinegar (or any other dressing of your choice) and toss to ensure the salad is coated. Fry the chopped bacon until starting to brown, then add to the salad. Poach the eggs (crack each egg into a separate cup; stir a large pot of simmering water vigorously to create a 'whirlpool' effect; slide egg into the whirlpool and cook for 2-3 minutes, or according to preference) then place on top of the bacon and salad. Serve in small bowls being careful not to puncture the yolk of the eggs – leave that fun for the eater! Great with bread and butter and a cup of tea or coffee.

German Buttermilk Waffles

Martina (mum to Gustav Josefsson)

MAKES APPROXIMATELY 12

I was born and raised in Germany, my husband Olof in Sweden. We try to keep both cultures alive in our family through language, festivals and traditions as well as typical food, which is why this popular German recipe is a favourite of ours. Waffles are perfect for weekend brunch, afternoon tea, kids birthday parties or even in the lunch box. We typically serve them hot, with a range of toppings, for example, fresh berries and whipped cream; maple syrup; jam; flavoured sugar (eg cinnamon); sliced banana. You can also add different flavours to the batter, for example, ground ginger or orange zest (good at Christmas time!).

125G BUTTER
50G CASTER SUGAR
1 PINCH OF SALT
1 TEASPOON VANILLA EXTRACT
4 EGGS
250G FLOUR
1 TEASPOON BAKING POWDER
250ML BUTTERMILK
VEGETABLE OIL OR BUTTER TO GREASE THE WAFFLE IRON

Pre-heat the waffle iron and grease with oil or butter (use a cooking oil spray or a pastry brush). Beat butter, sugar, vanilla, salt and eggs together until fluffy. Mix the flour and baking powder together and sieve into the egg mix. Stir to combine (do not over-mix), then quickly stir in the buttermilk. Drop one ladle of batter at a time onto the iron and cook for approximately 4-6 min until golden-brown and crispy.

Autumn

picnic

Make the most of the autumn sunshine: grab bikes, scooters and a few friends and head to the park! Most of these recipes can be made in advance and shoved in the freezer, making it easy to rustle up an impromptu picnic.

In Sweden this bun, 'Kanelbulle', is so popular that it even has a special day dedicated to it (4th October!). They are Bella and Enzo's favourite, and we always have some in the freezer, ready to pop in the oven. Delicious after school with a glass of cold milk, they also make a great picnic snack with hot chocolate when the weather turns cold. We sprinkle a special type of sugar on the top called Pärlsocker (coarse pearl sugar), which I usually bring back from Sweden with me, although it is possible to buy it in the UK from specialist stores and online. I also buy ground cardamom in Sweden, but you can grind the seeds in a pestle and mortar. I often use less sugar in the buns when I am making them for the children and they still taste great.

Swedish Cinnamon Buns

Cat (mum to Bella and Enzo Brown)

MAKES APPROXIMATELY 40

150G BUTTER, MELTED
500ML MILK
50G FRESH YEAST (OR
   EQUIVALENT IN DRY)
1/2 TEASPOON SALT
90G CASTER SUGAR
1/2 TEASPOON GROUND
   CARDAMOM
840-960G PLAIN FLOUR

FILLING INGREDIENTS:

100G BUTTER, SOFTENED
75G CASTER SUGAR
2 TABLESPOONS GROUND
   CINNAMON OR 1 TABLESPOON
   VANILLA SUGAR

TOPPING:
PÄRLSOCKER (COARSE PEARL
   SUGAR) OR FLAKED ALMONDS
1 EGG, BEATEN

Preheat the oven to 225°C/400°F/Gas Mark 6. Place paper muffin cases onto baking sheets. Melt the butter in a saucepan. Add the milk and heat to 37°C. In a large bowl, dissolve the yeast in a little of the milk, then stir in the rest along with the salt, sugar, cardamom and most of the flour. Mix until a dough forms and knead for 7-10 minutes by hand (or for around 5 minutes in a mixer with a dough hook) until dough is smooth and elastic. Leave to rise until doubled in size (30-45 minutes). Knead lightly on a floured surface (for up to 5 minutes) and divide into two equal parts. Roll out each section to a rectangle about 25 x 45cm. Spread with softened butter and sprinkle with sugar and cinnamon. Roll loosely from the long side, ending with the seam facing down, cut into buns and place in paper cases (this is important, or all the filling goes on the baking sheet and the buns go dry). Leave to prove for another 20 minutes, brush with a little beaten egg, sprinkle over the pärlsocker or flaked almonds and bake for 5-8 minutes. Leave to cool on a wire rack and cover with a tea towel. Any buns you're not planning on eating that day can be frozen as soon as they have cooled down, and reheated for 5-10 minutes in a warm oven (150°C/300°F/Gas Mark 2).

This recipe is taken from a favourite Swedish recipe book of mine. We use a lot of cardamom in Sweden, so our children are used to the taste. I buy ground cardamom (which I bring back from Sweden) but you can crush the seeds in a pestle and mortar. We love to take this hot chocolate with us on picnics (we take the cream in a jar, and give it a good shake for a minute or so before adding it). It's even nicer with a shot of dark rum!

Hot Chocolate with Cardamom

Cat (mum to Bella and Enzo Brown)

MAKES ONE LARGE CUP OR TWO SMALL ONES

1 TABLESPOON GOOD QUALITY
   COCOA POWDER
2 TEASPOONS LIGHT
   MUSCOVADO SUGAR
1/2 TEASPOON BLACK
   CARDAMOM SEEDS, CRUSHED
300ML MILK
50ML WHIPPING CREAM,
   LIGHTLY WHIPPED

Mix cocoa powder and muscovado sugar in a large cup. Heat the milk in a saucepan with the cardamom. Pour a little of the hot milk into the cocoa powder and sugar and stir until it forms a paste. Strain the milk, pour into the cup and mix. Top with lightly whipped cream and sprinkle with a little muscovado sugar.

Sausagemeat Pie

Wendy (mum to Sam and Zoe)

MAKES 8 SMALL PIES

This recipe (my Nana's) is really simple and not I guess really a recipe at all – just a glorified sausage roll – but it's a favourite in our household, and one of the first meals I made that we all ate (a truly eureka moment!). Each generation presents the pie slightly differently: my mum always does one big pie with a puff pastry topping, my sister makes a plait and I do individual pasty type pies with the initial of the recipient on it.

SHEET OF READY-MADE PUFF
PASTRY
450-500G SAUSAGEMEAT
SMALLISH ONION
MEDIUM CARROT
1 EGG
FLOUR FOR ROLLING
MILK FOR GLAZING PASTRY

Preheat the oven to 180°C/350°F/Gas Mark 4. Coarsely grate the onion and carrot and mix with the sausagemeat and egg until combined (I get stuck in with my hands!). Cut the slab of pastry in half and roll each half out on a lightly floured surface until roughly half a centimetre thick. Cut each piece of pastry into four squares and put some filling in a line along the middle. Make into rectangular pies by bringing top and bottom together over the filling and sealing the ends (press along the edges with a fork). Brush pastry with milk and cook for approximately 30 minutes until meat is piping hot and pastry golden. Can be eaten hot or cold.

Toffee Apple Flapjacks

Mrs Gill (Bishop Gilpin Teaching Assistant)

MAKES APPROXIMATELY 12

These are a Gill family favourite! They are not as quick to prepare as basic flapjacks, but worth the extra effort, and are excellent for Bonfire Night or Halloween parties. I am frequently asked by house guests if they can take a slice of flapjack and the recipe home with them! I have no idea where the recipe originally came from – I have been making them for years!

Preheat the oven to 180°C/350°F/Gas Mark 4. Grease and line a baking tin approximately 18 x 28cm. Heat the apples and lemon juice in a small pan and bring to the boil. Cover the pan and then simmer until the apple is just soft. Mash the apple with a fork and leave to cool slightly.

3 DESSERT APPLES (I USE COX
OR BRAEBURN) PEELED, CORED
AND CUT INTO SMALL CUBES
JUICE OF 1/2 LEMON
175G UNSALTED BUTTER
50G LIGHT BROWN MUSCOVADO
SUGAR
3 TABLESPOONS GOLDEN SYRUP
2 TABLESPOONS BLACK TREACLE
350G PORRIDGE OATS
150G TOFFEES
2 TABLESPOONS MILK

Place the butter, sugar, syrup and treacle in a pan and heat gently until the butter has melted. Remove from the heat and stir in the porridge oats until well combined. Place half the mixture into the prepared tin and press down firmly. Spread with the apple, then cover with the remaining flapjack mixture. Bake in the oven for 20-25 minutes or until golden-brown. Remove from the oven, cut into squares whilst still warm, then leave to cool completely in the tin.

While the flapjacks are cooling, unwrap the toffees and place in a small pan with the milk. Heat gently, stirring until melted and smooth. Drizzle the melted toffee mixture over the flapjacks. Cool in the fridge before serving.

Go Faster Banana Bread

The Speed family (Rosie and Erin)

MAKES 1 LOAF

This recipe - an amalgamation of about three different recipes - is really easy. We usually make a few at a time and then freeze them.

150G CASTER SUGAR
50G BUTTER
2 EGGS, LIGHTLY BEATEN
4 TABLESPOONS OF WATER
3 RIPE BANANAS, MASHED
200G WHOLEMEAL PLAIN FLOUR
1 TEASPOON BICARBONATE
1/4 TEASPOON BAKING POWDER
1/2 TEASPOON SALT (OPTIONAL)

Preheat the oven to 180°C/350°F/Gas Mark 4. Line a loaf tin with greaseproof paper. Cream the sugar and butter together until light and fluffy then mix in the eggs, water and bananas. Mix the dry ingredients together and incorporate gently into the wet ingredients. Spoon into the lined tin and bake for approximately 1 hour, until golden on the top.

Swedish Banana Cake

Lotta (mum to Jonas and Petra Bolton)

MAKES 1 18CM CAKE

This is my Swedish mother's recipe. She is an amazing cook and used to teach cooking for bachelors in the mid 1960s (that's how she met my dad!). My mum hates throwing food away and this recipe is great for using up bananas that are looking a bit sorry for themselves, as well as that last bit of crème fraîche or yoghurt that never seems to get eaten (which also makes it incredibly moist).

BREADCRUMBS (I WHIZZ UP TWO SLICES
   OF STALE BREAD IN THE FOOD PROCESSOR)
100G BUTTER OR MARGARINE
1 CUP CASTER SUGAR
2 EGGS
75ML HALF FAT CRÈME FRAICHE OR
   LOW-FAT YOGHURT
2-3 RIPE BANANAS, MASHED
1 TEASPOON VANILLA SUGAR
1 1/2 CUPS PLAIN FLOUR (NOT COMPACTED)
1 TEASPOON BAKING POWDER
1/2 TEASPOON BICARBONATE OF SODA

Preheat the oven to 175°C/350°F/Gas Mark 4. Grease a round or shaped 18cm cake tin, and cover with breadcrumbs. Melt the butter and let it cool a little. Whisk the sugar and egg, then add the melted butter, crème fraîche and bananas. Mix the vanilla sugar, flour, baking powder and bicarbonate of soda in a bowl and sieve into the wet ingredients. Gently stir until the flour is all mixed in, but be careful not to over-mix. Pour the mix into the tin and bake for approximately 40 minutes, or until a metal skewer comes out clean when inserted.

Apple Day is an annual celebration of apples and orchards. Apple-themed events take place across the country, in order to raise awareness of the richness and diversity of our local landscapes and help preserve them. Here in SW19, volunteers from Abundance Wimbledon organise Fruit Day, where there is delicious produce on offer made from local windfalls.

Apple day

Apple Sharlotka

The Patskov family (Misha, Dima and Marusia)

SERVES 6-8

This is a popular Russian recipe, usually cooked in autumn, the season of apples. It tastes even better the day after!

3 LARGE COOKING APPLES,
  PEELED, CORED AND
  SLICED INTO MEDIUM-
  SIZED CHUNKS, ABOUT
  1/2CM THICK
3 EGGS
1 CUP CASTER SUGAR (200-
  250G)
1 CUP PLAIN FLOUR (125G)
1/2 TEASPOON BAKING
  POWDER

Preheat oven to 180°C/350°F/Gas Mark 4. Line the bottom of a springform cake tin with greaseproof paper. Put apples into the tin. Beat the eggs and sugar together until they become a pale foam (this will take some time and is much easier using an electric mixer). Mix the flour and baking powder together and gently fold into the eggs and sugar. Completely cover the apples with the batter and bake in the oven for 30-40 minutes until the sharlotka is golden and an inserted skewer comes out clean. Cool in the tin for 10 minutes then place onto a wire cooling rack. Delicious warm with whipped cream, or cold.

Apples with Cinnamon

The Orrin family (Ruby, Lili and Lulu)

SERVES 4

Cinnamon always brings back happy memories of Greece – of time spent with the girls' great-grandmother from Athens, who lived to the grand old age of 98, and blissful summer holidays spent swimming in the clear blue waters of the Aegean. But the combination of apples and cinnamon – so warming and comforting – works perfectly on a chilly autumn day in England too! We like this simple but delicious pudding after a Sunday roast.

4 APPLES, CORED AND THINLY
  SLICED OR DICED
GENEROUS KNOB OF BUTTER
1/2 TEASPOON CINNAMON
1 TABLESPOON LEMON JUICE
SPRINKLING OF DEMERARA
  SUGAR

Heat the butter in a frying pan. Saute the apples over a low heat for 1-2 minutes until they start to soften. Sprinkle the apples with cinnamon and lemon juice. Continue cooking gently, until apples are soft and lightly browned and most of the liquid has evaporated (around 5 minutes). Arrange the apple slices on plates and sprinkle with the sugar. Serve while still warm. Delicious on its own or with cream, ice cream or custard.

season of mists and mellow fruitfulness! close bosom-friend of the maturing sun: conspiring with him how to load and bless...

...with fruit the vines that round the thatch-eaves run; to bend with apples...

Dutch Apple Pie
(Hollandse Appeltaart)

Pauline (mum to Sepp van der Plas)

YIELDS 10-12 SMALLER PIECES
OR 8 BIG SIZED ONES!

This is my Auntie Ariette's recipe. She is Dutch, but has lived in the UK for over 40 years now, and is famous locally for her apple pie. Traditionally, this pie is made with a Dutch variety of apples called Goudrenet, however you can easily use a mix of Bramley and Granny Smith, or similar.

FILLING:
1KG TART APPLES
JUICE OF 1 MEDIUM-SIZED
   LEMON
70G CASTER SUGAR
2 TEASPOONS GROUND
   CINNAMON
50G RAISINS

PASTRY:
175G UNSALTED BUTTER,
   AT ROOM TEMPERATURE,
   PLUS EXTRA FOR GREASING
   THE TIN
175G PLAIN FLOUR
175G SELF-RAISING FLOUR
175G CASTER SUGAR
1 LARGE EGG
1/2 TEASPOON LEMON ZEST,
   FRESHLY GRATED
1 TABLESPOON WATER
PINCH OF SALT

"MY FAMILY ARE FROM ENGLAND AND APPLE PIES REMIND ME OF ENGLAND. I EAT ONE A MONTH"

Lilac Jervis

1 TABLESPOON DRIED
   BREADCRUMBS
GROUND CINNAMON FOR
   SPRINKLING OVER THE TOP

Put the raisins in a small bowl along with a cup of hot water and let them soak for 15 minutes. Put the lemon juice into a bowl and start peeling, coring and cutting the apples into small pieces, placing them in the bowl as you go. Stir them around in the lemon juice every once in a while, so that they don't discolour. Drain the raisins, squeeze them with your hands and add them to the bowl along with the sugar and cinnamon. Mix well with a wooden spoon or spatula. Set bowl aside.

Preheat the oven to 180°C/350°F/Gas Mark 4. Grease the bottom and sides of a 22cm spring-form tin (7cm deep). In the bowl of a stand mixer (or in a large bowl), beat the butter on medium speed with the paddle attachment (or with your hand-held mixer), until softened and creamy, for 1-2 minutes. Sift flours directly into the bowl and add the sugar, salt, lemon zest, water and the egg. Mix all the ingredients with your hands and knead until you have a smooth, shiny, soft yet pliable dough that's not sticking to your hands. It will come together very quickly and easily. If it's too dry, add a teaspoon of water and if it's sticky, add a little bit of plain flour. Cut off a third of the dough and leave it aside.

Take the rest of the dough, shape it into a ball and place it in the middle of the spring-form tin. Using the back of your hand, press the dough over the bottom and up the sides of the pan. The dough should come up to ⅔ of the height of the tin. Try to spread the dough as evenly as possible. Sprinkle the base of the pastry case with the dried breadcrumbs, so that the base doesn't become soggy from the juice of the apples. Mix the filling once more with a spoon, drain the juice (it will make the pie soggy) and empty the filling into the tin. It should fill the whole pastry case. Take the piece of dough you left aside and divide it into smaller pieces. Roll each piece into long, thin round strips and use them to decorate the tart, lattice style. Brush the pie dough with some egg or milk to give it a glossy look. Place the tin on the middle rack of the oven and bake for 45-50 minutes, until the crust takes on a golden-brown colour. Allow the pie to slightly cool inside the tin and then remove the sides of the tin and move the pie onto a platter or cake stand.

The pie is eaten either warm or at room temperature. Serve with a dollop or two of whipped cream or a scoop of vanilla ice cream, and sprinkled with a little ground cinnamon.

Apple, Pear and Vanilla Compote

Jean-Jacques Lescure, from Abundance Wimbledon

MAKES 10 SERVINGS

Abundance Wimbledon is an organisation, set up in 2011, which aims to use up surplus fruit in Wimbledon. There are lots of fruit trees in the local area, but much of the fruit falls to the ground and is wasted. In the last three years we have picked nearly 4 tonnes (that's 3,900 kg), much of which has been made into jams and chutneys, or else baked, preserved and frozen. And we have given around 1,200 kg away to local charities. Find out what we're up to at www.abundancewimbledon.com, or come along to our annual Fruit Day.

Compote, or mashed stewed fruit, is the simplest way to use local fruit at home. Peel and chop 500g pears and 500g apples and place in a saucepan with 50ml of water. Add 100g sugar, the juice of the quarter of a small lemon and a hint of vanilla. Cook over a gentle heat for 10-15 minutes, then mash in the saucepan with a masher or even a fork and you have your compote! As simple as that! This compote will keep for a week in the fridge. It can be made in smaller quantities, for instance one apple and one pear will make a good serving. Delicious eaten slightly warm, topped with a spoon of Cornish double cream and a shortbread biscuit.

Here's another idea for using up some of the bounty available at this time of year:

Wimbledon Common Clafoutis

Bernie Phillips (dad to Lara and Theo)

SERVES 4

This is a real shortcut pud, but tastes great all the same. It's so easy, even the children can make it.

```
MEDIUM TUB OF BLACKBERRIES
LARGE KNOB OF BUTTER, MELTED
   (APPROXIMATELY 60G)
1 1/4 CUPS CASTER SUGAR
1 CUP SELF-RAISING FLOUR
1 CUP MILK
SUGAR FOR SPRINKLING
```

Firstly, go for a walk on the common in September armed with suitable containers. We employ our own children to pick the juiciest blackberries but I am sure you can rope in willing harvesters of any age. Back home, preheat the oven to 180°C/350°F/Gas Mark 4, and grease a medium-sized oven-proof dish. Wash and pat dry blackberries (don't let the children do this unless you want them squished!). Get children to whisk butter, sugar, flour and milk to make the batter. Pour batter into the dish and spread blackberries evenly over the top. (Don't put too many in as it will make the end result too gooey). The blackberries dissolve so it will be lovely and moist. Bake for an hour, then sprinkle on a thin layer of sugar and bake for a further 5 more minutes until the top turns golden. Serve with cream!

...the mossed cottage trees. and fill all fruit with ripeness to the core... BY JOHN KEATS

There are often crowds to feed at this time of year, with all sorts of feasts and festivals bringing people together, including Diwali, Eid, St Martin's Day, Bonfire Night and Halloween. What better food for gatherings of friends and families than fragrant pots of curry and exotic stews, with authentic accompaniments (perfectly cooked rice, yoghurt based sauces, flatbreads)? We also have some yummy crowd-pleasing puds, and some ideas for Bonfire Night and Halloween.

Autumn Feasts and festivals

"WE DECORATE THE HOUSE A FEW DAYS BEFORE WITH FLOWER DECORATIONS. WE EAT INDIAN SNACKS AND WE HAVE A FEAST FOR DINNER."

Kiran Tandon

"MY FAMILY CELEBRATES A SPECIAL DAY CALLED EID. WE SHARE THINGS AND GIVE THINGS."

Ammar Hasan

"WE CELEBRATE EID WITH A LOT OF LAUGHTER, JOY AND ENJOYMENT. WE ALSO HAVE JOKES AND OUR ELDERS GIVE US CLOTHES, TOYS AND MONEY."

Saira Abedi

Caramel Chicken

Eliza (mum to Kalle Ward)

SERVES 2

This tasty Chinese meal is so easy to make I often make it for family and friends if they visit when I don't have time to spend hours preparing a meal. My Chinese grandmother taught my German mother how to cook Chinese food when my parents moved to Kuala Lumpur. My mother was shown how to shop for fresh local ingredients at the markets: which vegetables to buy and how to choose the best live fish and chickens that she would return for once they had been butchered to her requirements. My mother dictated this recipe to me from memory. Her skill and experience with Chinese cooking is such that she cooks many of her dishes by 'feel' — it's a dash of this or a slurp of that. I have done my best to translate this recipe into one with measured ingredients.

4 CHICKEN LEGS OR THIGHS
1-2 CLOVES GARLIC, FINELY CHOPPED
2 TABLESPOONS OIL (A GOOD FRYING OIL LIKE PEANUT OR GRAPESEED OIL)
40G WHITE SUGAR
10ML DARK SOY SAUCE
1-2 STAR ANISE (DO TO TASTE: I USUALLY USE 2)

MARINADE:
15ML (1 TABLESPOON) LIGHT SOY SAUCE
PINCH BLACK PEPPER (GROUND SZECHUAN PEPPERCORNS CAN BE USED INSTEAD FOR A NICE ALTERNATIVE)
PINCH SALT (TASTE BEFORE ADDING AS SOY SAUCE IS SALTY)

Coat the chicken pieces with the marinade and leave for 30-60 minutes. Heat the oil on a medium heat in a wok or similar deep pan then add the sugar and stir until it is brown and caramelised. The oil and sugar will separate as the sugar caramelises, but don't worry about this. Add the chicken, star anise, garlic and dark soy sauce and cook over a gentle heat, turning the chicken pieces occasionally, until the chicken is cooked (about 30-40 minutes) and the surrounding sauce is a dark brown/black colour. Don't let the sauce get too reduced or it will stick and burn. Add a little water as you go if necessary. Remove the star anise, garnish with parsley sprigs and serve with a steamed white rice, such as jasmine, long grain or basmati. This recipe is very accommodating. Virtually each time I make it I scour my fridge for ingredients that need using up and throw them in, for example spring onions, mushrooms or peppers.

Veal in Cream and Mushroom Sauce (Geschnetzeltes)

Britta (mum to Frederik and Ella Blom)

SERVES 4

The dish with veal or pork is popular throughout Germany. Ideal for the busy cook, it takes only 30 minutes to make. It is served with rice or egg noodles, and is perfect for parties, as people can serve themselves.

800G VEAL OR PORK TENDERLOIN, CUT INTO THIN STRIPS ABOUT 2 INCHES LONG
200G MUSHROOMS, SLICED
150G ONIONS, FINELY DICED
250G SINGLE CREAM
125ML DRY WHITE WINE
2 TEASPOONS PLAIN FLOUR
BUTTER, FOR FRYING
SALT & PEPPER

Dust meat with flour. Heat the butter in a frying pan and brown the meat on all sides, then transfer to a plate and set aside. Saute the onions and the mushrooms until tender, then add the white wine. Simmer for a few minutes then add the cream and return the meat to the sauce. Give a good stir and add salt and pepper to taste. Goes well with carrots or mange tout.

This delicious stew, a typical dish served at feasts, is one of my Iranian grandmother's recipes. I don't get to see her very often, and we don't even speak the same language, but food provides us with a way of connecting. During her visits to the UK over the years we have spent many happy hours together in the kitchen - me keen to learn about my Persian heritage, and she - patient and smiling - happy to share her wisdom.

One thing I have learned about Persian feast food is that the most important ingredients are the friends and family with whom the food is to be shared, a sentiment I'm keen to pass on to my son Christian, just as my family has passed on to me.

Iranian Duck, Walnut and Pomegranate Stew (Khoresht Fesenjān)

Afsana (mum to Christian Short)

SERVES 4-6

4 DUCK LEGS AND 4 DUCK
    THIGHS
500G WALNUTS
1 TEASPOON TURMERIC
BLACK PEPPER TO TASTE
400G POMEGRANATE
    CONCENTRATE
3 TEASPOONS SUGAR
3/4 MUG OF HOT WATER

Place the duck pieces in a saucepan, cover with boiling water and simmer gently for 30 minutes, topping up with more hot water if necessary. Meanwhile, toast walnuts in a large frying pan on a high heat (taking care not to burn them) for a couple of minutes, put into a blender and blitz until a fine paste is formed (like peanut butter). Season with the turmeric and pepper then add to the saucepan with the duck. Mix the pomegranate concentrate with the sugar and hot water, add to the pan and give a good stir. Continue to simmer for about an hour, until the oil in the walnuts is released, the colour turns to a deep rich brown, the mixture becomes thick and the duck is tender. Dilute with hot water if the sauce is too thick, and serve with rice.

why not try with persian rice?
see page 38

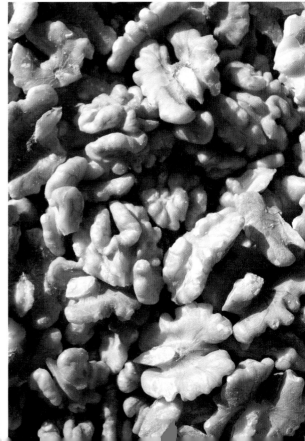

Lamb Biryani

Ambreen (mum to Zain Vellani)

SERVES 3-4

Biryani is a special dish which I usually make for celebrations, such as the festival of Eid. It is very popular in the Indian sub-continent and each region and family has its own recipe which has been handed down from generation to generation. This is my mother-in-law's recipe, who learned it from her mother-in-law. It's quite involved, but once the ingredients are all prepared the dish is fairly quick to assemble and you will feel very proud of the end result! I usually buy the pure ground chilli powder and the garlic and ginger pastes from an Indian store, but chilli powder from the supermarket makes an acceptable substitute, as do, of course, fresh garlic and ginger.

1KG WHITE BASMATI RICE
4 LARGE ONIONS, FINELY SLICED
3 MEDIUM POTATOES, PEELED AND
    CUT INTO QUARTERS
VEGETABLE OIL

FOR THE GARAM MASALA POWDER:
2-3 STICKS CINNAMON, BROKEN
    IN HALF
SEEDS FROM 2 CARDAMOMS
2 WHOLE CLOVES
2 TO 3 WHOLE PEPPERCORNS

1/2KG LAMB SHOULDER, CUT INTO
    SMALL CUBES (OR CHICKEN)
1 STICK CINNAMON BROKEN IN
    HALF
2 CARDAMOMS PODS
2 CLOVES
2 OR 3 WHOLE PEPPERCORNS
250G NATURAL YOGHURT (LIGHTLY
    BEATEN)
1 SMALL ONION, FINELY SLICED
1 TOMATO, CHOPPED
1 TEASPOON GINGER PASTE (OR
    FINELY CHOPPED FRESH GINGER)
1 TEASPOON GARLIC PASTE (OR
    CRUSHED FRESH GARLIC)
JUICE OF HALF A LEMON
1/2 TEASPOON RED CHILLI POWDER
    (OR ACCORDING TO TASTE)
1/2 TEASPOON TURMERIC
1 TEASPOON SALT (OR ACCORDING
    TO TASTE)
FEW STRANDS OF SAFFRON SOAKED
    IN WARM WATER (ABOUT 2 TO 3
    TABLESPOONS)

Wash the rice by covering with water in a large bowl and giving it a good stir with your hand. Drain and repeat the process several times. Simmer rice in a pan of water for about 5 minutes until it has started to soften but still retains some bite. Drain and set aside. Fry the onions until they are golden-brown and crispy. In a separate pan, fry the potatoes until they are nicely browned. Meanwhile, grind together the ingredients for the garam masala (I use an electric coffee bean grinder, but a pestle and mortar is fine) and store in a jar.

Place a saucepan large enough to take the cooked meat and rice together on a medium heat. Add the meat to the saucepan with the cinnamon, cardamom, cloves, peppercorns, yoghurt, lemon juice and the onion (no water added). Stir well and simmer for about 30-40 minutes for lamb or about 20 minutes for chicken. Then add the garlic, ginger, tomato, chilli powder, turmeric and salt. After a few minutes add 1-1½ teaspoons of the garam masala, the potatoes and the onions (keep some onions for later). Let it all cook for a few minutes then add the rice, which should sit on top of the sauce. Make holes in the rice with the back of a spoon and pour in the saffron water, which will create a yellow and white marbled effect. Sprinkle the remaining fried onions on top of the rice, then put the lid on and turn the heat down quite low. After 5 to 10 minutes open the lid and the biryani is ready to eat. Serve with Raita (page 39).

Green Chilli Chicken

The Sugiarto-Tandon family (Kiran)

SERVES 5

This is a special Indonesian dish which we serve with yellow rice (see page 38). If you're not a big fan of spicy food, then omit the chilli. I usually separate some for Kiran as she's not a fan of anything spicy (although we're secretly hoping that will change when she's older!). I've put an asterisk next to the ingredients that are available in Asian supermarkets (for example Wing Yip), with alternative options in brackets. Any unused ingredients can be frozen and will keep for months.

```
1/2 KG CHICKEN BREAST, IN BITE-SIZED CHUNKS
2 TABLESPOONS TAMARIND WATER * (OR SUBSTITUTE
   WITH LIME JUICE OR 1/2 TEASPOON TAMARIND
   PASTE DILUTED WITH WATER)
5 KAFFIR LIME LEAVES*
1/2 TURMERIC LEAF*

SPICE PASTE:
6 HAZELNUTS (TOASTED OVER
   A LOW HEAT)
1/2 LEMON GRASS STICK
3 CLOVES GARLIC
1/2 RED ONION
1 TABLESPOON GALANGAL * (GINGER)
1 TEASPOON TURMERIC POWDER
1 TEASPOON FRESH GINGER
1 TEASPOON GROUND BLACK PEPPER
   (USE LESS IF YOU DON'T LIKE IT HOT)
250G GREEN CHILLI, SEEDS REMOVED
   (USE LESS/OMIT ALTOGETHER IF YOU
   DON'T LIKE IT HOT)
1-2 TEASPOONS SALT
2 TEASPOONS OIL
```

Blend all the paste ingredients together and cook on a low heat for around 5 minutes to bring out all the flavours. Add the chicken, tamarind water, lime leaves, turmeric leaf and 250ml water. Simmer gently until the chicken is cooked. Remove the leaves and serve with rice (page 38) and spinach or cucumber.

A karahi is a type of cooking pot, traditionally used in Pakistan to cook dishes made from a base of tomatoes and green chillis, simmered for a long time until they are really rich and tasty. My mother used to make this dish but I follow my mother-in-law's recipe, which is easier. This dish is often cooked for feasts and festivals and I've never met anyone who doesn't like it. The recipe uses a ginger and garlic paste, which I buy from the Asian stores in Tooting. Making it fresh is not difficult, but it's time consuming so as I use it on daily basis I normally buy a 500g jar, which lasts us for a month or two. It's easy to make in bulk at home though: just grind garlic and ginger in a ratio of 2:1 in a food processor with little water and store in a sterilised jar. The paste will keep for 3-4 weeks (it may turn slightly green after a day due to oxidation as we are not using preservatives).

Lamb Karahi

Roohi (mum to Imaan Tausif Awan)

SERVES 4

500G LAMB (I NORMALLY USE LEG).
   DICED INTO SMALL CUBES
VEGETABLE OIL
1 TABLESPOON GINGER AND GARLIC PASTE
   (OR 2 GARLIC CLOVES AND A SMALL
   PIECE OF GINGER CHOPPED FINELY)
4 MEDIUM-SIZED TOMATOES. CHOPPED
2 GREEN CHILLIES. CHOPPED
FRESH CORIANDER LEAVES & JULIENNED
GINGER FOR GARNISHING

Heat some oil in a pan and sauté the ginger and garlic paste and the lamb for half a minute then add the tomatoes, chillies and salt. Cook on a low to medium heat for approximately 40-45 minutes until the meat is tender. Garnish with the coriander leaves, green chillies and julienned ginger, and serve with naan and Raita (page 39).

Bengali Fish Curry

Pallavi (mum to Neha and Shreya Sinha)

SERVES 4

This is a recipe from West Bengal, a state in the Eastern region of India, where my family is from. It was given to me by my friend's mum, although not with quantities - we use our senses when cooking. It's quite a dry curry (you won't have puddles of sauce), but it's a delicious and aromatic way to serve fish. Fresh fenugreek (methi) is sold in bunches from Asian stores (I buy mine in Tooting). It is very fragrant and has many medicinal properties. If you can't get hold of fresh fenugreek you can substitute it with frozen chopped methi, or dried fenugreek powder. Add the dried fenugreek at the same time as the other spices.

300-400G FISH FILLETS (FRESH OR
   FROZEN - WE USUALLY USE FRESH WATER
   FISH, BUT ANY WHITE FISH WORKS WELL)
1 TABLESPOON TURMERIC
1 TEASPOON SALT
1 BAY LEAF
SMALL PIECE OF CINNAMON STICK
1 TEASPOON GINGER PASTE
1 ONION, FINELY CHOPPED
1-2 TABLESPOONS VEGETABLE OIL
1 TABLESPOON TOMATO PUREE
1 BUNCH FRESH FENUGREEK LEAVES,
   FINELY SLICED (OR 1 TEASPOON DRIED
   FENUGREEK)

Cut the fish into small pieces and rub with turmeric and salt. Heat oil in a wide, shallow frying pan. Add the bay leaf, cinnamon stick, onion and ginger paste, and fry until onion is lightly brown. Add the tomato purée and fry till oil is released. Add the cut fenugreek and fry. To this add the cut fish pieces and then turn the gas to low and cook the fish in the masala turning occasionally. Add hot water, a little at a time, if necessary. Enjoy with roti (see page 36) or rice (see page 38).

Chicken Curry

Naseem (mum to Louis Walker)

SERVES 4

This is my mum's own recipe for chicken curry. This is a very typical dish from Mumbai, where she grew up. She's been making it for us as a family since coming over from India 40 years ago, and has passed on the recipe to me and my sister, whose own families and friends get to enjoy this dish now too. Louis, our five year old, always asks for it, and it was a silent approving nod to my now husband when he managed to eat two whole platefuls of it on first meeting my family!

2 CHICKEN BREASTS, CUT INTO SMALL PIECES
2 MEDIUM ONIONS, FINELY CHOPPED
1 TEASPOON CUMIN SEEDS
2 TABLESPOONS VEGETABLE OIL
2 TABLESPOONS TOMATO PUREE
2 CLOVES GARLIC, CRUSHED
2 TEASPOONS GINGER PASTE (AVAILABLE
   FROM MOST SUPERMARKETS)
FRESH GREEN CHILLIES, FINELY CHOPPED (OPTIONAL)
2 TEASPOONS GROUND CORIANDER
2 TEASPOONS GROUND CUMIN
1 TEASPOON CHILLI POWDER
2 TEASPOONS ALL SPICE
1 TEASPOON TURMERIC
2 TABLESPOONS NATURAL YOGHURT
SALT
CORIANDER LEAVES, TO GARNISH (OPTIONAL)

Fry the onion in the oil with the cumin seeds until golden-brown. Add the diced chicken and fry on a medium heat to brown and then add all the remaining ingredients.
Turn up the heat and stir well to prevent the yoghurt curdling. Add 120ml water and mix well, then simmer for 20-25 mins until the chicken is tender. If you prefer a curry with more sauce, add some puréed plum tomatoes and simmer until the desired consistency is reached. Garnish with fresh coriander leaves. Good with lime pickle!

 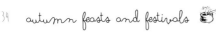

Chapati (Roti)

Wajeeha Iqbal (mum to Maryam Iqbal)

· SERVES 4

Chapati, or roti, as it's known in Pakistan, is a healthy flatbread which we eat daily with curry. It can be made from many different types of wheat flour (atta), for example, white, wholemeal or chakki (a mix of wholemeal and white), as well as other grains such as gram flour and corn flour. My grandmother taught me how to make roti, and I will teach my daughters in a few years time. We often make them in advance and keep them in the fridge. Whenever I make dough to prepare making roti, the girls love to play with the atta.

2 CUPS WHOLEWHEAT FLOUR
(WE USE 'PILLSBURY'
CHAKKI ATTA. AVAILABLE
IN BIG SUPERMARKETS)
SALT TO TASTE
1/2 CUP WATER

Combine the flour and salt in a bowl. Add the water and mix to make a dough then knead well until smooth (about 10 minutes). Cover the dough and let it stand for 30 minutes then divide the dough into balls. Sprinkle with flour and flatten then roll out each ball into a 12cm (4.5in) round chapatti. Stretch it in your hands to make it bigger (see photo). Heat up a heavy frying pan until a drop of water in it sizzles. Pick up one chapati and lay it in the frying pan. Cook for about 40 seconds till the surface of the chapati puffs. Turn it over and cook for about 30 seconds, pressing down with a spoon so that the chapatti puffs up. It's done when it puffs up. Stack the cooked chapattis together, wrapped in a clean tea towel, and serve hot with curry.

this is how chapatis are made

Flatbread

Jane (mum to Nick and Michael Long)

This recipe (from the DK Children's Baking Book) is brilliant. I started looking at bread recipes when I got fed up with buying extortionately priced dough balls, then we graduated onto flatbread. You can make it before you pick the kids up, leave to prove and then it's ready to go at tea-time. I promise you'll never buy packet pittas again!

250G STRONG WHITE FLOUR
1 TEASPOON FAST ACTION DRIED YEAST
1/2 TEASPOON CASTER SUGAR
1/2 TEASPOON SALT
175ML LUKEWARM WATER (I DO ABOUT ONE THIRD
BOILING WATER. TWO THIRDS COLD)

Place flour, yeast, sugar and salt in a large mixing bowl and mix well with a wooden spoon. Make a well in the centre and stir in enough of the water to form a soft dough. Place the dough on a lightly floured surface and knead for 5 minutes until smooth and elastic. Return dough to the bowl and cover with a clean damp tea towel. Leave in a warm place for an hour or until doubled in size. 'Knock back' the dough (punch it with your fist) to remove the large air bubbles and then divide the dough into six equal chunks with your hands. Knead each chunk lightly on a lightly floured surface to make a flatter round shape. Then roll out each piece of dough into a 13cm circle with a rolling pin. Pre-heat a frying pan. Add a flat piece of dough and cook for a minute until golden underneath. Then flip it over and cook the other side for 30 seconds. Serve immediately.

Persian Rice (Polow or Polo)

Afsana (mum to Christian Short)

For Persians, making rice – the staple of our cuisine – non-sticky is considered an art form. We tend to use basmati or long grain rice and I highly recommend investing in a simple rice maker! There are different variations; this dish, *polow*, is normally served with kebabs or stews. Wash rice twice and soak in salted warm water for 3-4 hours, then drain. Half-fill a large non-stick heavy-bottomed pan with water and bring to the boil. Add rice and a spoonful of salt and continue boiling until rice slightly softens. Pour rice into a sieve and wash with slightly warm water. Pour a few spoonfuls of cooking oil into the pan and add rice. Pour a few more spoonfuls of oil over rice. Cover the pan and cook over low heat for about half an hour. If cooking time is increased, a delicious and prized crispy layer of rice (known as the *tahdig* ('ta-deek') will form at the bottom of the pan.

Vegetable Pilau Rice (Pulao)

Pallavi (mum to Neha and Shreya Sinha)

Wash and soak 1½ cups of white basmati rice in water for one hour. Peel and slice 2 medium onions. Wash and chop 3-4 tomatoes. Peel 2 small carrots and dice them into half-inch cubes. Cut 12 or so fine beans into half-inch pieces. Heat 3 tablespoons ghee (or olive oil) in a thick-bottomed pan. Add 1 teaspoon cumin seeds, 3 green cardamom pods, 4 large black cardamon pods and 5 cloves. Once spices start to crackle, add sliced onions and cook till onion becomes translucent. Add chopped tomatoes and cook till oil can be seen on the sides of the pan. Add salt to taste and 3 cups of water and bring to the boil. Add carrots and cook for 5 minutes. Drain excess water from the rice and add to the pan. Once it starts to boil, add ½ cup green peas and ½ cup cauliflower florets, diced beans and salt. Reduce the heat, cover pan and cook till rice is completely done. Before serving lightly stir to remove any lumps.

Perfect Basmati Rice

The Vellani family (Zain)

Making perfect rice is an art itself. Each grain has to be cooked and look fluffy. Wash the rice by covering with water in a large bowl and giving it a good stir with your hand. Drain and repeat the process several times. Take a large pan and add 2 measures of cold water to 1 measure of rice. Bring to the boil, reduce to a low heat and simmer for 10-12 minutes with the lid on until the water is absorbed and the rice is soft. Avoid opening the lid or stirring the rice. Remove from heat and allow to stand for a few minutes.

Yellow Rice

The Sugianto-Tandon family (Kiran)

Yellow rice is the foundation of Indonesian *nasi tumpeng*, a dish prepared for celebrations. The rice is shaped into a cone, surrounded with side dishes and then the top part presented to the most-respected guest, for example, at a child's birthday party the child would present it to his or her parents. Ideally you should use Thai rice which is long and fat (the opposite of basmati rice) and is slightly sticky (but not as sticky as Japanese sushi rice), but feel free to use any rice that you have. I've put an asterisk next to the ingredients that are available in Asian supermarkets (for example Wing Yip). Any unused ingredients can be frozen and will keep for months. This rice is delicious with Green Chilli Chicken (page 31). Wash 500g rice, then add to a saucepan with 650ml coconut milk,1 tablespoon turmeric powder, 1 pandan leaf *, 1 lemon grass stick *, 2 lime leaves* and 1 teaspoon salt. Cover and cook on a low heat, stirring frequently, until the rice is cooked. Serves 5.

Persian Yoghurt and Cucumber (Maast-o-Khiar)

Afsana
(mum to Christian Short)

SERVES 6
(OR 4 GREEDY PEOPLE!)

This is a very simple side dish, great with most dishes or delicious on its own. Mix 500g natural yoghurt, ½ grated cucumber, 2 finely chopped spring onions, 2 crushed garlic cloves, 3 tablespoons dried mint and salt and pepper to taste. Best made the night before, so the flavours have time to develop.

Raita

The Vellani family (Zain)

SERVES 4-6

Toast 1 teaspoon cumin seeds in a frying pan, taking care not to burn them, then crush in a pestle and mortar. Add to 2 cups lightly beaten natural yogurt, ½ chopped cucumber and a few chopped mint leaves. Raita is ready!

Frangelico Tiramisu

Emma (mum to Alice and Sam Helbert)

SERVES 12

This tiramisu is boozy, so definitely one for the adults, but it's delicious and a real crowd pleaser for a special celebration. It is also incredibly easy, and can be made in advance (1-2 days if kept in the fridge, or up to 3 months if frozen). If freezing, wrap the tiramisu (without its topping of hazelnuts and cocoa) in a double layer of clingfilm and foil, then defrost overnight in the fridge and add topping before serving.

```
250ML ESPRESSO COFFEE (OR 8 TEASPOONS ESPRESSO
   POWDER DISSOLVED IN 250ML BOILING WATER)
250ML FRANGELICO HAZELNUT LIQUEUR PLUS MORE
   FOR FILLING (SEE BELOW)
2 EGGS. SEPARATED
75G CASTER SUGAR
60ML FRANGELICO LIQUEUR
500G MASCARPONE
APPROX 375G SAVIORDI BISCUITS (FINE SPONGE FINGERS).
   DEPENDING ON SIZE OF DISH USED
100G ROASTED HAZLENUTS. CHOPPED
3 TEASPOONS COCOA POWDER
```

Combine the coffee and 250ml Frangelico liqueur and allow to cool if coffee is hot. Beat the egg whites until frothy. In a separate bowl, beat the yolks and sugar with 60ml Frangelico. Add the mascarpone to the yolks and sugar mixture, and mix well. Gently fold in the foamy egg whites and mix again. Pour half of the coffee and Frangelico mixture in to a wide shallow dish and soak the biscuits (they should be damp but not falling to pieces). Line a square dish (24 x 24cm) with a layer of soaked biscuits, pouring over any leftover liquid you have from soaking the biscuits.

Put half the mascarpone mixture on top of the soaked biscuits and spread to make an even layer. Pour the remaining coffee and Frangelico mixture into the shallow dish and make another, final layer of biscuits (soaked as before). Pour any leftover liquid over the biscuit layer and finish with the final layer of mascarpone. Cover with cling film and leave overnight, or for at least 6 hours in the fridge. When you are ready to serve, mix the chopped hazlenuts with 2 teaspoons of the cocoa powder and sprinkle this over the top layer of mascarpone. Then sieve the final teaspoon of cocoa powder over the top, to give a light dusting.

Deer's Back

Nada (grandmother to Emily Douglas)

MAKES ONE LOAF

This cake brings back many fond memories (not least being young and surrounded by all my family!). I come from Belgrade in Serbia. During the Second World War, food was scarce and the ingredients to make cakes like this were unavailable. This cake seemed like an unimaginable treat.

Some years later when it was possible to buy chocolate and butter again, my mother was able to resume baking. She used to make Deer's Back during the winter months and at Christmas. The name probably comes from its appearance, as, with a little imagination, the chocolate coating resembles the back of a deer!

Deer's back

Ingredients:
- 100 gr. butter
- 150 gr. sugar
- 150 gr. ground walnuts
- 100 gr. chocolate
- 6 eggs
- 3 tablespoons breadcrumbs
- a little rum
- grated orange peel
- some apricot jam
- Sainsbury's chocolate covering.

Method:

Mix well butter and sugar; add egg yolks; mix well; add melted chocolate and breadcrumbs previously soaked in rum. Add ground walnuts, egg whites previously well beaten and finally grated orange peel. Mix well. Transfer the mixture into a long mould lined with a baking sheet and bake for about 40 minutes at 180°C.

Take the cake out of the oven and let it cool. Then spread some apricot jam over it and pout Sainsbury's chocolate covering on top of the jam.

Bon appétit!

mrs wardell's
Black Forest Cake

Jackie Wardell
(Bishop Gilpin Office Administrator)

SERVES 12

This a retro style dessert which is a firm favourite with all my family, especially for special celebrations!

200G UNSALTED BUTTER,
  SOFTENED, PLUS EXTRA
  FOR GREASING
125G SELF-RAISING FLOUR
5 TABLESPOONS COCOA POWDER
2 TEASPOONS BAKING POWDER
5 LARGE FREE-RANGE EGGS,
  SEPARATED
150G CASTER SUGAR
2 TABLESPOONS MILK
100G 70% COCOA CHOCOLATE,
  MELTED, PLUS 50-100G
  TO SERVE

FOR THE BOOZY CHERRIES:
250G PITTED FRESH CHERRIES,
  OR CHERRIES FROM A JAR
  (DRAINED WEIGHT)
50ML KIRSCH OR BRANDY
3 TABLESPOONS CASTER SUGAR
GRATED ZEST OF 1 ORANGE
  (OPTIONAL)

FOR THE CHANTILLY CREAM:
500ML DOUBLE CREAM
50G CASTER SUGAR
1/2 VANILLA POD, SPLIT
  LENGTHWAYS AND SEEDS
  SCRAPED

Preheat the oven to 150°C/300°F/Gas Mark 2. Grease and line a round cake tin (roughly 20cm). Sift the flour, cocoa powder and baking powder together; set aside. In a large, very clean bowl, whisk the egg whites to firm peaks using an electric beater. In another bowl, cream the butter and sugar until pale and fluffy. Beat in the yolks one at a time, then stir in the milk, then the melted chocolate. Fold the flour into the chocolate mixture, then stir in one big spoonful of egg white to loosen. Fold the rest of the egg white through the chocolate mix until just incorporated. Pour into the cake tin and bake for 50-60 minutes, until a skewer inserted into the middle emerges clean. Cool for 5 minutes and then turn out onto a wire rack. Leave to cool completely.

To make the boozy cherries, set aside a few cherries for garnish, then put the rest in a pan with the sugar, kirsch or brandy and orange zest, if using. Bring to a simmer over a gentle heat and cook till the cherries are just soft but holding their shape. Leave to cool. For the Chantilly cream, whisk the cream, sugar and vanilla seeds into soft peaks.

To assemble the cake, cut the cake horizontally into 3 rounds, using a long, sharp knife. Drizzle each cut side with the syrup from the cherries to moisten. Place the bottom round on a cake stand, spread with the Chantilly cream and dot with half the cherries. Place the middle layer of the cake on top and repeat with more cream and cherries. Top with the last layer of cake, then spread cream on the top and the sides too, if you like. Top with the reserved cherries and some dark chocolate shavings. You can soak the cherries in orange juice if you would prefer not to use alcohol

"SOMETIMES IF WE ASK HER A QUESTION AND SHE
DOESN'T KNOW THE ANSWER THEN SHE TELLS US TO COME
BACK TOMORROW AND THEN SHE SOMETIMES LOOKS ON THE
INTERNET OR HAS AN ADVENTURE AND THE NEXT TIME
WE MEET HER SHE TELLS US THE ANSWER."

"MRS WARDELL IS A REALLY KIND LADY
AND SHE HAS A GOOD HEART AND EVERY
TIME SOMEONE ASKS HER A QUESTION
SHE ANSWERS IT WITH A GENTLE VOICE."

A fan of Mrs Wardell

43

Halloween ideas

"ME AND MY FAMILY CELEBRATE HALLOWEEN BY EATING MONSTER CUP CAKES."

Charlize Bueter

Halloween cupcakes

The Hopkinson family (Lauren and Ellie)

Make a batch of cupcakes and buttercream icing using Elaine's recipe on page 88, then decorate using the options below.

GHOST CUPCAKES:
TUBE OF SMARTIES
SMALL TUBE OF BLACK ICING

Place two same-coloured Smarties onto each cupcake and add dots of black icing to make eyes. (Chocolate sprinkles or any other black sweets could be used instead.) Set aside for 20 minutes to allow the icing to harden.

SPIDER'S WEB CUPCAKES:
25G/1OZ ICING SUGAR
1 TABLESPOON COCOA POWDER

Sift icing sugar and cocoa powder into a bowl. Stir in 2 tablespoons of water to form a smooth, thick icing. Transfer the mixture to a piping bag with a fine nozzle. (Alternatively, spoon the mixture into the corner of a sandwich bag and snip off the corner, to form a small hole). Carefully pipe 3 concentric circles onto each cupcake. Run a toothpick from the centre to the edge of the cake, through each circle of icing, at 2cm/1in intervals to create a cobweb effect.
Set aside for 20 minutes to allow the icing to harden.

"MY FAMILY CELEBRATE HALLOWEEN AND WE EAT FISH PIE WITH GARLIC BREAD BECAUSE WHEN YOUR WHOLE FAMILY IS ROUND YOU NEED TO BAKE A SIMPLE BUT BIG MEAL."

Georgina Williams-Ellis

Severed Fingers

Break some flaky breadsticks in half and stick a flaked almond on each one with cream cheese to make a finger nail. Dip end of breadstick into raspberry jam.

Halloween Sandwiches

Using Halloween-themed cookie cutters cut sandwiches into appropriate shapes. If having a party, use a different shape for each kind of sandwich

Graveyard Jellies

Make up a packet of lime jelly according to packet instructions. Put a small handful of 'gummy worms' or other small Halloween-themed sweets into a clear glass or jar. Cover with the jelly and leave in a fridge to set.

For those who don't like the 'trick or treat' principle, or the way Halloween celebrates fear and darkness, but who love the idea of the community coming together to have fun, a 'Light Party' might be a good idea.

Sticky Maple-Apple Traybake

Bethan Jenkins (Youth Worker at St Mark's Church)

MAKES 20 PIECES

This is a fantastic apple recipe which I made recently for our toddler group at St Mark's and it went down a storm! Adapted from 'The Great British Bake Off', by Linda Collister with Mary Berry and Paul Hollywood, it's also perfect when there are crowds of hungry children and teenagers to feed. The original recipe used 50g walnut pieces (added at the same time as the apple mixture), which I leave out when baking for children.

FOR THE CAKE:
400G BRAMLEY APPLES.
3/4 TEASPOON GROUND CINNAMON
2 TEASPOONS MAPLE SYRUP
125ML SUNFLOWER OIL
150G LIGHT BROWN MUSCAVADO
   SUGAR
1/2 TEASPOON VANILLA EXTRACT
GRATED ZEST OF 1/2 LEMON
2 LARGE EGGS
50G WALNUT PIECES
275G PLAIN FLOUR
1/2 TEASPOON BAKING POWDER
1 TEASPOON BICARBONATE OF SODA
GOOD PINCH OF SALT
2 LARGE EGG WHITES, AT ROOM
   TEMPERATURE

FOR THE TOPPING:
75G UNSALTED BUTTER,
   SOFTENED
75G LIGHT BROWN
   MUSCAVADO SUGAR
3 TABLESPOONS MAPLE
   SYRUP
175G FULL-FAT
   CREAM CHEESE

Preheat the oven to 180°C/350°F/Gas Mark 4. Grease and line a traybake tin (20.5cm x 20.5cm x 5cm). Place the apples, cinnamon and maple syrup in a bowl and stir to combine.
In a separate bowl whisk together the oil, sugar, vanilla and lemon zest (this is easier with an electric mixer). Add the eggs and whisk for a couple of minutes until the mixture has thickened and has a mousse-like consistency. Stir in the apple mixture, then carefully fold in the flour, baking powder, bicarbonate of soda and salt – the mixture will be quite stiff. Put the egg whites into another bowl and whisk until stiff peaks form. Fold into the apple mixture in 3 batches. Transfer the mixture to the tin and distribute evenly.
Bake for 30-35 minutes or until golden-brown and a skewer inserted into the centre of the cake comes out clean.

> AT ST MARK'S WE THROW A 'LIGHT PARTY' EVERY YEAR — SILLY GAMES AND YUMMY FOOD GUARANTEED!
> Bethan Jenkins

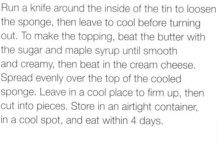

Run a knife around the inside of the tin to loosen the sponge, then leave to cool before turning out. To make the topping, beat the butter with the sugar and maple syrup until smooth and creamy, then beat in the cream cheese. Spread evenly over the top of the cooled sponge. Leave in a cool place to firm up, then cut into pieces. Store in an airtight container, in a cool spot, and eat within 4 days.

Toffee Apples

Tristan Hopkinson (mum to Lauren and Ellie)

MAKES 6

6 APPLES
300G CASTER SUGAR
2 TABLESPOONS GOLDEN SYRUP
JUICE OF 1/2 LEMON

Wash the apples and push a lolly stick or skewer through each one. Put the sugar, syrup and 150ml water into a heavy pan over a low heat. Simmer until the toffee turns a golden colour. Remove from heat and carefully add the lemon juice. Dip each apple into the toffee and swirl it around to cover. Sit the apples on baking paper to dry. Eat the same day.

Crunchy Toffee

Jane Lyons (Taken from the first Bishop Gilpin cookbook, edited by Barbara Zarzycki and Rose Williams, July 2002).

This toffee is absolutely irresistible and is ready to break up and eat almost straight away.

2 TABLESPOONS GOLDEN SYRUP
1 TABLESPOON GRANULATED SUGAR
1 LEVEL TEASPOON BICARBONATE OF SODA

Stir the golden syrup into the granulated sugar on a very low flame in a wetted 6 inch saucepan. When the sugar melts boil the mixture for 5 minutes, stirring. Remove from the stove and stir in the bicarbonate of soda. It will foam deliciously! When it has stopped foaming pour the mixture on to a buttered tin.

It's Bonfire night!

Keep warm on Bonfire Night with steaming bowls of pumpkin soup, bacon pasties and the ultimate chilli, followed by some classic English sweet treats.

Spicy Pumpkin Soup

Laura (mum to Sam Hynes)

SERVES 4-8

1 MEDIUM PUMPKIN
2 MEDIUM SIZE ONIONS, CHOPPED
2 CLOVES GARLIC, FINELY CHOPPED
2 TEASPOONS DRIED THYME
1 TEASPOON CUMIN
2 PINTS OF GOOD VEGETABLE STOCK
  BUTTER AND OLIVE OIL
SALT AND PEPPER, TO TASTE

Preheat the oven to 190°C/375°F/Gas Mark 5. Halve the pumpkin, remove seeds and skin, cut into chunks and place on a baking tray. Drizzle with olive oil, season with salt and pepper and sprinkle over the thyme. Bake for about 25 minutes, until soft. In a saucepan, heat a knob of butter and a drizzle of olive oil and add onion. Cook on a low heat until soft, then add garlic and cumin and stir for a minute or so, being careful not to let the garlic brown. Add pumpkin and stock and simmer together for a few minutes. Take off the heat and let it cool a little before blitzing with a hand-held blender or in a food processor.

Bacon Pasties

Vicky Williams-Ellis (mum to Georgina and Bella)

MAKES 8

My mother gave me this recipe and she inherited it from her mother-in-law. As far as I know, it's a one-off: I've never met anyone who has come across it before. The pasties can be eaten hot or cold. We've used them for winter picnics or bonfire night parties, wrapping them in tin foil to keep them warm.

500G SHORT CRUST PASTRY
1 LARGE ONION, CHOPPED
6 RASHERS OF BACON,
  CHOPPED
6 BUTTON MUSHROOMS
  (OPTIONAL), CHOPPED
1 SMALL TIN OF BAKED BEANS

Preheat the oven to 180°C/350°F/Gas Mark 4. Fry the onion, bacon and mushroom until the bacon is crisp. Add the beans and mix thoroughly. Roll out the pastry and cut it into rounds (using a small saucer as a guide). Spoon the filling into the middle of each circle. Brush the edges of the pastry with a little milk, then bring them up to the middle, pinching at the top to make a pasty. Brush them with a beaten egg and cook for about 20 minutes or until golden-brown.

remember, remember the fifth of november, gunpowder, treason and plot...

This is a fantastic chilli recipe. I ripped it out of a magazine, but I've long since lost the page, so have no idea where it originally came from! It has a bit of a 'kick' to it, but it's not too hot for my children. As it's quite rich I tend to cook it when we have friends to stay for the weekend It's great served with rice or tortilla chips with sour cream.

The Ultimate Chilli

Julie (mum to Harry and Freddie Haynes)

SERVES 4-6

OLIVE OIL
1KG BRAISING OR STEWING
  STEAK, CUT INTO CHUNKS
200G CHORIZO, SLICED
2 ONIONS, CHOPPED
4 GARLIC CLOVES, FINELY
  CHOPPED
2 TEASPOONS GROUND ALLSPICE
2 TEASPOONS GROUND CUMIN
1 TEASPOON CAYENNE PEPPER
1 BAY LEAF
1 MEDIUM DRIED CHILLI (CHOPPED)
3 TABLESPOONS BALSAMIC
  VINEGAR
2 TABLESPOONS SUGAR
2 TABLESPOONS KETCHUP
2 X 400G TINS CHOPPED TOMATOES
200ML RED WINE OR STOCK
30G DARK CHOCOLATE, GRATED
1 X 400G TIN KIDNEY BEANS,
  DRAINED
SALT AND PEPPER

Preheat oven to 140°C/275°F/Gas Mark 1. Heat the olive oil in a frying pan or casserole dish and brown the steak. Set aside. Lightly brown the chorizo and set aside. Add a little extra olive oil to the chorizo oil, add the onions cook gently until softened. Add the garlic, spices, bay leaf, chilli, balsamic vinegar, sugar, ketchup and tinned tomatoes and season. Put the meat and chorizo back in the pan, stir together, then add red wine and grated chocolate and bring to simmering point. Transfer to the casserole dish if not already and cover. Cook in the oven for 2 hours. After this time, add the kidney beans, then return to the oven and cook for a further 45-60 minutes. Top with chopped fresh coriander and serve with tortilla chips, sour cream and rice.

...i see no reason, why gunpowder treason...

Rutland Gingerbread

Gill Williams (mum to Elsie)

MAKES APPROXIMATELY 10 SLICES

A visit to Elsie's Granny in Rutland always involves a pot of tea and a freshly baked cake. This Gingerbread is one of her best. It's not necessarily a traditional food of Rutland, but when you come from the smallest (and best) county, it is important that you give it a mention whenever you can! I am afraid I don't know the origin of this recipe – it's been hand-written on scraps of paper for decades. This cake keeps very well for about a week, and also freezes well, but in our family, we tend just to eat the lot as quickly as we can...

8 OZ BUTTER OR MARGARINE
8 OZ SOFT BROWN SUGAR
4 OZ BLACK TREACLE
4 OZ GOLDEN SYRUP
12 OZ PLAIN FLOUR
2 LEVEL DESSERTSPOONS
GROUND GINGER
3 TEASPOONS GROUND
  CINNAMON
2 BEATEN EGGS
2 LEVEL TEASPOONS
  BICARBONATE OF SODA
1/2 PINT MILK

Preheat oven to 150°C/300°F/Gas Mark 2. Line two 2lb loaf tins. Melt the butter, treacle, syrup and sugar. Sift the flour and spices into a bowl. Stir the melted mixture into the flour, and add the beaten eggs. Mix thoroughly. Heat the milk until it is luke-warm and add the bicarbonate to it. Pour into the mixture and stir until it is well mixed. The mixture will be surprisingly runny for a cake. Pour evenly into two loaf tins and bake for approximately one hour until a tester comes out cleanly from the middle. The tops of the cakes will crack but if they look like they are beginning to burn, cover with foil until the cakes are baked through. Turn onto a rack to cool.

Grandma's Bonfire Night Treacle Tart

The Womack family (Grace)

SERVES 8

BG Grandma Kitty, 81, has made this dish literally hundreds of times for family and friends, and first made it with her own mother 65 years ago. Cake sparklers and a 'Guy Fawkes' figure placed on top add the magic.

9 OZ SELF-RAISING FLOUR
PINCH OF SALT
3 OZ CHILLED COOKEEN
  (HARD, NOT FROM A TUB)
4 OZ CHILLED MARGARINE
  (AS ABOVE)
2 TABLESPOONS COLD WATER
12 OZ GOLDEN SYRUP
8 OZ FRESH WHITE
  BREADCRUMBS (NO CRUSTS!)
1/4 TEASPOON LEMON JUICE

Sieve flour and salt together into a large bowl. Add Cookeen and margarine in small pieces. Rub together with fingertips until the mixture resembles fine breadcrumbs. Sprinkle water on to make a soft pliable dough and use a round edged knife to mix together. Wrap dough in cling film and leave to chill in the fridge for 30 minutes.

Preheat the oven to 200°C/400°F/Gas Mark 6. Gently heat the syrup in a saucepan until it goes soft and melts, and stir in the breadcrumbs and lemon juice. Retrieve the pastry from the fridge and roll it out to fit a 9-10 inch loose-bottomed flan tin. Line the flan tin with the pastry, and put the cooled syrup and breadcrumbs mixture into the pastry, in the tin. You should have enough pastry left to make trellis strips for the top of the tart. Roll out the leftover pastry in an oblong shape to make them. Fasten the strips to the tin edges and crimp the edges of the pastry to join the trellis with the flan tin, and brush tart edges and trellis lightly with milk. Pop in the oven for 10 minutes, and then reduce the oven temperature to 180°C or gas mark 4 and bake for a further 25 minutes or until the pastry is golden and the filling is firm.

...should ever be forgot.

merry Christmas

Christmas in Denmark by Dorthe Hermansen

Christmas in Denmark is a lovely time. It is cold and dark outside, but very inviting inside, with all the Christmas lights and decorations, and lots of delicious baking smells wafting out of the kitchen! We start celebrating on the first Sunday of Advent, when we gather together with friends and family to light the first of four candles on our special advent candle, and share biscuits, sweets and a glass or two of glögg (similar to mulled wine). It is also a tradition for families to share the Christmas workload by getting together to make biscuits, marzipan figures and Christmas decorations.

twas the night before christmas... when all through the house... not a creature was stirring... not even a mouse...

BY WILLIAM

In Denmark, we celebrate Christmas Eve on December 24th. The main meal - duck or turkey with various side dishes is eaten in the evening. For dessert we always have *Ris a la mande* which is a kind of rice pudding mixed with almond pieces and whipping cream and served with cherry sauce. There is one whole almond in the bowl and the person who finds it gets a present. After the dinner we gather round the Christmas tree to light candles and sing carols, which we do whilst walking around the tree. Finally, all the waiting is over for the children and presents can be opened!

Vanilla Sugar Cookies (Sofus Vanilladreams)

Dorthe (mum to Amelia and Sofie Hermansen)

MAKES APPROXIMATELY 60 COOKIES

> 200G LIGHTLY SALTED BUTTER,
> SOFTENED
> 100G CASTER SUGAR
> 2 TABLESPOONS VANILLA SUGAR
> 1/2 VANILLA POD, SPLIT LENGTHWAYS
> WITH THE SEEDS SCRAPED OUT
> 225G PLAIN FLOUR
> 1/2 TEASPOON BAKING POWDER

Preheat the oven to 180°C/350°F/Gas Mark 4. Line 3 baking sheets with greaseproof paper. Cream butter, sugar, vanilla sugar and vanilla for approximately 10 minutes. Then add flour and baking powder and stir gently until the mix forms a soft dough. Roll dough into small balls, place on a baking tray with a decent space in between each one and flatten them using a fork dipped in flour. (The dough will be easier to work with if it has been left in the fridge for a bit before rolling them into balls). Bake in the oven for approximately 15 minutes.

Danish Honey Biscuits

Dorthe (mum to Amelia and Sofie Hermansen)

MAKES APPROXIMATELY 50 BISCUITS

360G PLAIN FLOUR
200G HONEY
90G CASTER SUGAR
1 LARGE EGG
1 TABLESPOON GROUND
 CINNAMON
1 TABLESPOON GROUND GINGER
1 TABLESPOON GROUND CLOVES
1 TABLESPOON BICARBONATE
 OF SODA

Preheat the oven to 180°C/350°F/Gas Mark 4. Line 3 baking sheets with greaseproof paper. Warm the honey in a pan. Put the sugar in a bowl and stir in the honey. Leave to cool for a little while. Whisk the eggs together and add to the honey/sugar mixture together with the spices, bicarbonate of soda and flour. Mix the dough together. Roll the dough out to a thickness of approximately half a centimetre and cut out different shapes. Make a hole in the cakes using a toothpick if you would like them to hang on the tree. Place on baking tray and bake for 10-12 minutes. Decorate the cakes with icing sugar, sprinkles, Smarties etc.

Danish Peppernuts

Dorthe (mum to Amelia and Sofie Hermansen)

MAKES APPROXIMATELY 150

This crunchy cookie is a favourite
at Christmas. When it arrives in the shops you
know that Christmas is not far away!

250G CASTER SUGAR
250G SLIGHTLY SALTED BUTTER,
    SOFTENED
500G PLAIN FLOUR
1 TEASPOON GROUND GINGER
1 TEASPOON CINNAMON
1 TEASPOON WHITE PEPPER
1 TEASPOON GROUND CARDAMOM
1 TEASPOON BAKING POWDER
1 TEASPOON BICARBONATE OF SODA
100ML SINGLE CREAM

Preheat the oven to 180°C/350°F/Gas Mark 4. Line 2-3 baking
sheets with greaseproof paper. Cream butter and sugar for
approximately 5 minutes. Add flour and spices and finally the
cream. The dough needs to be firm enough to roll. Roll into
long thin sausages (the thickness of a little finger). Cut into small
pieces, about 1in thick, place on a baking tray and bake for
10-12 minutes. It's important that the peppernuts are baked
enough, or they won't be crunchy.

peppernuts in the making

Christmas Klejner

Dorthe (mum to Amelia and Sofie Hermansen)

MAKES APPROXIMATELY 50

These are little deep-fried twists - delicious!

250G PLAIN FLOUR
65G CASTER SUGAR
65G BUTTER, SOFTENED
1 EGG
75 ML SINGLE CREAM
1/2 TABLESPOON BAKING POWDER
VEGETABLE OIL, FOR FRYING

Mix flour and baking powder together, then add the other ingredients and mix well to a smooth dough.
Rest in the fridge for approximately 30 minutes. Roll the dough out to a thickness of approximately
5-7 mm and cut into rectangles approximately 5 x 2 cm (I use a cutter but you can use a knife). Make
a little cut in the middle of each rectangle and twist one of the ends through the hole. Fill a large
saucepan or wok with vegetable oil to a depth of approximately 2-3 cm and heat the oil until it sizzles
when a small piece of dough is dropped in. Deep fry the klejner in batches of about x until they are
golden brown on each side, turning half-way through. Leave to cool on a piece of greaseproof paper.

Coconut Balls

Dorthe (mum to Amelia and Sofie Hermansen)

MAKES APPROXIMATELY 30

These are very quick and fun for the children to make.

```
150ML PORRIDGE OATS
125ML DESICCATED COCONUT
50ML ICING SUGAR
2 TABLESPOONS UNSWEETENED COCOA
60G BUTTER, SOFTENED
1/2 TEASPOON VANILLA SUGAR
2 TABLESPOONS DOUBLE CREAM
```

Mix all the ingredients together and roll into small balls, approximately 3cm in diameter. Roll in desiccated coconut and leave to harden slightly in the fridge for at least one hour before eating.

Peppermint Bark

Carolina (nanny to Olivia & Charlie Graham)

MAKES 5-6 JARS

I have been linked with the Bishop Gilpin community for the last four years, and through my work as a nanny have met lots of nannies and mums who I have become very good friends with. Every year I try to make peppermint bark and give it away as little gifts.
It's good for teachers too!

```
10 X 100G BARS DARK CHOCOLATE
10 X 100G BARS WHITE CHOCOLATE
4 TABLESPOONS PEPPERMINT
  EXTRACT
5 CANDY CANES
```

Line a medium baking tray with greaseproof paper. Melt the dark chocolate by breaking it into a large heatproof bowl and placing over a saucepan filled with a couple of inches of water. Heat gently, stirring occasionally to ensure the chocolate doesn't burn. When melted, spread the chocolate evenly over the tray then refrigerate for about 30 minutes. Repeat the melting process with the white chocolate, using a clean bowl. Meanwhile, break the candy canes into small pieces by placing in a freezer bag and smashing with a rolling pin. When the white chocolate has melted, stir in the peppermint extract and spread over the baking tray, making sure the dark chocolate is completely covered. Finally, sprinkle over the candy cane and refrigerate for a final 30 minutes. When hardened, chop into pieces and wrap in nice paper and ribbon.

Baking these more-ish biscuits has been a Christmas tradition in my German mother's family for many generations. Elsie was my grandmother's eldest brother's wife, who lived to be almost 100. One of my favourite childhood memories is making them with my grandmother, mother and sisters to give away in jars we had hand painted. Even the milkman received a jar from us every year! I can still remember the spicy sweet smell of our kitchen piled high with containers of dough ready for a marathon baking day just before Christmas. Our all-time baking record was about 1,300 biscuits from five batches of dough in one very l-o-n-g day.

My grandmother had a huge collection of cutters which she had bought in Germany, some of which must have been 30-40 years old at the time. Our favourite was Father Christmas with a sack on his back, but we were banned from making too many of those by our mother because his feet often broke off! We also used shapes like dogs, bones, chickens, ducks and so forth. The mixture can be made in advance and kept in the fridge or freezer, and the biscuits keep for several months in an airtight container.

Great Aunt Elsie's Honey Jumbles

by Eliza (mum to Kalle Ward)

MAKES ABOUT 250 BISCUITS DEPENDING ON THE SIZE

1 1/2 LBS (750G) HONEY
APPROXIMATELY 4 1/2 LBS (2KG) PLAIN FLOUR
1/4 CUP WATER (250ML CUP MEASURE)
3/4 LB (375G) DARK BROWN SUGAR
2 EGGS
4 TEASPOONS BICARBONATE OF SODA
1 TEASPOON GROUND CLOVES
1/2 TEASPOON ALLSPICE
1/2 TEASPOON NUTMEG
1/2 TEASPOON CINNAMON
EXTRA EGG & MILK TO GLAZE

Preheat the oven to 180°C/350°F/Gas Mark 4. Line baking sheets with greaseproof paper. Warm the honey and water then add the brown sugar and mix well. When cool add the eggs, bicarbonate of soda, spices and sufficient flour to make a stiff dough. Knead the dough with extra flour until it is dry enough to be rolled without sticking to a floured rolling pin or to the cookie cutters. Roll out to a thickness of about half a centimetre and cut out the biscuits with your favourite cookie cutter shapes.

Place on baking trays, glaze the biscuits with a mixture of egg and milk, and bake for 10-14 minutes, swapping top and bottom trays halfway through cooking if necessary, until the biscuits have increased in size and have browned slightly. Once cool the biscuits can be iced but they are just as delicious plain.

Tablet is like a very sweet, hard fudge. I grew up eating this but I don't ever remember seeing it in a shop; it was always homemade or found on the cake stalls at Highland Games and fêtes etc. This is a family recipe which we make for family gatherings and which has been tweaked over the years (for example, Great-Great-Aunt Peggy used water instead of milk; there is a version with treacle instead of sugar). You can experiment with flavourings such as a few drops of vanilla, whisky or ginger (just add to the mix when you remove from the heat before whisking). Tablet tastes nice when just made but is actually better after a day or two because it keeps hardening.

Scottish Tablet

Rhona (mum to Oliver Pryor)

MAKES APPROXIMATELY 16-20

125G UNSALTED BUTTER
1KG CASTER SUGAR
300ML FULL FAT MILK
PINCH OF SALT
200ML CONDENSED MILK

Grease a 23 x 33cm swiss roll tin or equivalent. Put the butter in pan and melt over a low heat (you will need a very large heavy based pan as the mixture can easily double in size, and if the heat is a fraction too high it will rise up quickly and boil over). Add sugar, milk and salt and heat gently until the sugar has dissolved, stirring occasionally. Bring to the boil and simmer over a fairly high heat for about 8-10 minutes, stirring often (make sure you get into the corners of the pan as it can stick). Add the condensed milk, stir well then simmer for anything from 10-30 minutes until the mixture reaches the 'soft ball' stage. If you have a thermometer it will be around 114°C-115°C, but usually I go by the ball test (ie the mixture forms a soft ball which you can roll between your fingers when a little is dropped into a cup of very cold water). Start testing as soon as the colour starts to darken (a bit like the colour of a Dime bar). Immediately remove from the heat, stir in any flavourings if required, and, using an electric hand whisk, beat at medium speed for about 4-5 minutes until the mixture begins to stiffen and becomes ever so slightly grainy. (You can do this by hand but it is hard work!). Immediately pour into the buttered tin, and when cool, cut into squares or bars. Store in airtight tin or wrap in individual pieces of grease proof paper.

NB It is important to wait for the ball point otherwise the tablet will not set hard. It can take anything from 10-30 minutes to get there so don't worry if it seems to be taking forever!

Anyone who knows me will vouch for the fact that I love good food and family gatherings, so I get really excited about Christmas every year as it's always a time when everyone makes the effort to be together. Nowadays one of my daughters usually cooks on Christmas Day, but I like to make the traditional pudding which my family always demands (but is usually too full to eat until the next day)! In the days when the church calendar drove the pattern of feasting and fasting in this country, it was customary to make the pud on the last Sunday before the season of Advent, a day in November known as 'Stir-up Sunday'. Tradition dictates that an old-fashioned sixpence is placed in the mixture ('for good luck') and each member of the family has a stir.

This recipe, which I have used for over 20 years, is based on one given to me by my dear friend Marilyn. The grated carrot makes it moist and the barley wine (a traditional English ale – not a wine! – available in major supermarkets) gives it a lovely flavour. The pudding is steamed for five hours (filling the house with a delicious Christmassy scent), and then needs to be wrapped up and kept in a cool place until Christmas for all the flavours to develop. It is then steamed for an hour or so before eating (to warm through). It's customary to flame the pudding with brandy, then serve warm, with thick cream or custard, or – my favourite – brandy butter. Any leftovers can be microwaved, but are even more delicious fried with a little butter in a pan (gooey and crisp!).

Maggie's Christmas Pudding

Maggie (grandma to Evie and Grace Barrett)

MAKES TWO PUDDINGS (EACH SERVES 6-8)

225G SULTANAS
225G RAISINS
550G CURRANTS
200G GLACE CHERRIES
100G MIXED PEEL
110G GRATED CARROT
GRATED RIND OF 1 ORANGE
GRATED RIND OF 1 LEMON
4 TABLESPOONS DARK RUM
1 CAN (300ML) BARLEY WINE
4 EGGS
200G VEGETABLE SUET
200G WHITE BREADCRUMBS
110G SELF-RAISING FLOUR
450G SOFT BROWN SUGAR
1/2 TEASPOON GRATED NUTMEG
50G CHOPPED ALMONDS
OPTIONAL: 2 SIXPENCES
   (CLEAN THOROUGHLY AND
   EAT WITH CAUTION TO
   AVOID CHOKING!)

Grease two, 2 pint ceramic or plastic pudding basins. Mix all the fruit together in a large mixing bowl with the rum and barley wine, cover with a clean tea towel and leave overnight for the fruit to absorb the liquid and become juicy and plump. The next day, beat the eggs together and add to the fruit. In another bowl mix the remaining ingredients together, then stir thoroughly into the fruit, getting everyone in the household to have a turn! Fill each pudding basin with mixture, pop a sixpence into the depths of each pudding then cover with plastic lid or double layer of greaseproof paper tied on tightly with string. Make a pleat in the grease-proof paper before tying, if using, to allow for expansion. Place each pudding into a large saucepan and fill up to halfway with boiling water. Cover and steam for around 5 hours, until cooked through, keeping the pans topped up with boiling water so they don't boil dry. Remove puds from pan, (I place a long piece of foil folded into a sturdy rectangle underneath the puds before cooking, to serve as a 'handle'), leave to cool, re-cover with dry greaseproof paper (if using ceramic bowls) and store in a cool place until ready to eat. Steam for one hour to warm through before serving, then turn out onto a plate, top with a sprig of holly and a couple of tablespoons of warmed brandy and set alight at the table (the holly should be fine, even if it catches alight!).

Yummy 'Never Fail' Cheese Souffle

Jemma (mum to Abby Poole-Robb)

SERVES 4 (OR 3 HUNGRY PEOPLE)

This soufflé does not have to strike fear into your heart, as it is indeed a never fail, most utterly scrumptious dish. Although the French invented soufflés, my family has been using this recipe for over a hundred years, and we come from the heart of Africa! It works no matter what cheese you use, in which oven-proof dish you bake it, or in which continent you live! I have no idea where the recipe came from but my grandmother (and I believe her mother too), and my mother, made the dish weekly. For best results, prepare in advance and leave for up to 18 hours in the fridge before baking. (I will often make it in the morning, keep it in the fridge and bake it in the evening). We like to serve it with a tomato salad.

6 LARGE EGGS
6 OZ (180G) CHEESE (WE
   USUALLY USE CHEDDAR)
3OZ (90G) BUTTER OR
   MARGARINE
3OZ (90G) PLAIN FLOUR
1 TEASPOON SALT
1/2 TEASPOON PAPRIKA
A DASH OF CAYENNE PEPPER
3/4 PINT (412ML) FULL-FAT
   MILK

Butter a large ovenproof soufflé dish. Grate the cheese. Separate the eggs and set to one side in two bowls. Melt the butter in a saucepan over a gentle heat, then stir in the flour and seasoning and cook for several minutes. Add the milk all at once and cook, stirring constantly until the mixture is smooth and thickened. Add cheese and stir well. Gradually stir the egg yolks into the cheesy mixture, blending thoroughly. Take off the heat. Beat egg whites stiffly and gradually pour the cheesy mixture over them, folding carefully until all the egg has been amalgamated. Pour into the prepared soufflé dish, place in cold oven and bake for 45 minutes at 200°C/400°F/Gas Mark 6, until well risen and crisp and brown on the top. You could 'kill' it by inserting a skewer into its middle and if comes out clean, then it's cooked. But if it is a huge, brown, wonderful smelling pillow, it's done! Serve immediately, whilst it is high and looking beautiful!

"ON CHRISTMAS DAY WE USUALLY GET GUESTS AND WE MAKE LAMB CHOPS, A SELECTION OF PICKLES, COUSCOUS, SALAD AND WE HAVE A PREPARED DESSERT MAYBE CUSTARD OR SOMETHING LIKE THAT."

Nikolai Harin

"I EAT RICE PUDDING QUITE OFTEN AT CHRISTMAS BECAUSE WE THINK THE HEAT OF RICE PUDDING HELPS US WARM UP OUR DAY."

Erin Verwoord

Grandma's Christmas Eve Fish Pie

Ali (mum to Tom and Sophie McGrath)

SERVES 6

Tom and Sophie's Grandma always makes fish pie for supper on Christmas Eve and we have adopted the tradition. None of the ingredients is particularly Christmassy, but its appearance always signals the start of Christmas for us. It tastes good at other times of year too!

750G POTATOES, PEELED AND
   CUT INTO CHUNKS
900G OF A COMBINATION OF
   SALMON FILLETS (SKINNED),
WHITE FISH FILLETS (SKINNED)
   AND COOKED, PEELED PRAWNS
5-10 BLACK PEPPERCORNS
1 BAY LEAF
425ML MILK, PLUS EXTRA
FOR TOPPING
30G BUTTER, PLUS EXTRA
   FOR TOPPING
30G PLAIN FLOUR
1 TABLESPOON FRESH PARSLEY
   OR DILL, CHOPPED
JUICE OF 1/2 LEMON
2 TABLESPOONS DOUBLE CREAM
   OR APPROXIMATELY 50G
CHEDDAR CHEESE, GRATED
SALT AND BLACK PEPPER, TO
   TASTE

Preheat the oven to 180°C/350°F/Gas Mark 4. Cook the potatoes in boiling water, until softened, then mash with butter and milk, to taste. Place the fish fillets in a pan, with the milk, peppercorns and bay leaf and poach over a low heat until the fish is just cooked through. Do not overcook. Remove the fish fillets from the poaching liquid and flake into an ovenproof dish (make sure to remove any bones), retaining the liquid. Remove the peppercorns and bay leaf. Melt the butter in a pan and add the plain flour. Keep stirring the mixture for a couple of minutes, then gradually add the poaching liquid and stir, over a low heat, until smooth and thickened. Add the chopped parsley or dill, the lemon juice and the double cream or grated cheese and season, to taste. Put the prawns and flaked fish into the dish and pour over the sauce. Place the cooked potato on top of the fish mixture and make a textured pattern on the top, with a fork. Dot the top of the pie with thumbnail-sized pieces of butter, then place in oven for approximately 30 minutes or until the top is brown and crispy. Warburton family tradition dictates that this pie is always served with peas, but you can serve it with any vegetables you like.

Vin Chaud

Gregor (dad to William Robertson)

MAKES 4-6 GLASSES

When I left university I decided that a brief spell in the Alps would do me the world of good educationally, so I packed my bag and headed out to the French ski resort of Val d'Isere. Twelve years later I finally moved back to the UK, having set up a bar and restaurant business which still continues today (albeit it from South West London). I learnt a lot over the years, mostly inappropriate for a recipe book, but one thing that may be of interest was our Vin Chaud recipe. There are many regional and national variations to a good glass of vin chaud/ glühwein/mulled wine, but when we were catering for hundreds of chilled and weary skiers, there was no time for finesse! The main ingredient is red wine and apologies to anyone who may have paid 15 francs for a glass at the time, but the cheapest wine is the best!

1 BOTTLE RED WINE
1 1/2 TABLESPOONS BROWN
   SUGAR
1/2 TEASPOON GROUND CINNAMON
25ML LEMON JUICE (EITHER
   FRESHLY SQUEEZED OR FROM
   A BOTTLE)
1 SLICE ORANGE, TO SERVE

Simply heat up the wine slowly adding the ingredients and stir. I always told my staff to heat it gently as people couldn't drink it fast enough but I do believe that bringing it to the boil will also impair the taste. Serve in a toughened glass preferably with a handle, or a mug, and add a slice of orange. Goes very nicely with roast chestnuts (see recipe on page 66).

These tasty little home-made Christmas treats are thus named because Nelly's dad, uncle and aunt used to say they were like eating bullets when they were young. They might have thought they were like bullets, but there are never any left when all the guests have departed after Christmas! Granny used to make them with Nelly's older cousins but, now they are far too old to be around before Christmas, Nelly helps Granny. Because Granny uses ready-made products this is a really quick way of providing delicious Christmas fare.

Granny's Bullets (otherwise known as Mince Pies!)

The Boydell family (Nelly)

MAKES 12

1 X 500G PACK OF SHORT
   CRUST PASTRY (READY-
   ROLLED IS EASIEST)
FLOUR, FOR ROLLING PASTRY
350G MINCEMEAT
1 EGG IF USING (AS GLAZE
   AND FOR SEALING THE
   BULLETS)
ICING SUGAR, FOR DUSTING

Preheat the oven to 160°C/325°F/Gas Mark 3. Roll out the pastry (if un-rolled) on a lightly floured surface. Cut circles that will fit in a cake tin (or 'patty tin' as Granny calls it). Grease the holes of the tin and add a circle of pastry to each. Re-roll the pastry and cut out smaller circles for the top of each 'bullet.' Place a dessertspoon of mincemeat in each pastry circle. Wet around the top of each circle (with a beaten egg or with water if you're being really speedy) and place a smaller circle on each one. Pinch around the edges to seal them. Pierce the top of each bullet to allow the steam to escape whilst cooking and brush with the remaining egg yolk,

if you used it and if you'd like your bullets to be a little shiny when cooked. Cook in the oven for about 40 minutes but check them after 30 minutes. Allow to cool on a wire rack when cooked and dust with icing sugar.

Roast Chestnuts

Gregor (dad to William Robertson)

Chestnuts can be bought in the supermarket or greengrocers and to cook you simply make a cross in the top with a knife and roast in the oven (or over a fire or barbecue) for around 20 minutes until they open. It's important that they are crossed as otherwise they can pop with quite a considerable force!

Raisin Sauce for Ham

Rebecca (mum to Eva McKenzie)

SERVES 4

This recipe was given to me by my mother, Mary Davis, who lives in Denver, Colorado. She clipped it out of an American newspaper sometime during the late 1960s/early 1970s. My mother made this sauce often when serving ham, as do I, as it's so quick and easy and tastes delicious.
As the recipe is American, you will need suitable measuring cups and spoons.

1/4 CUP RAISINS
1 1/4 CUPS WATER
1/4 CUP BROWN SUGAR,
   PACKED
1 TABLESPOON CORNFLOUR
   (US CORNSTARCH)
2 TABLESPOONS BALSAMIC
   VINEGAR
1 TABLESPOON BUTTER
   OR MARGARINE

Rinse and drain raisins. Put raisins and water in a saucepan and simmer for 5 minutes. Blend sugar and cornflour in a bowl and add gradually into raisin mixture, stirring continuously. Continue stirring over a low heat until the mix is clear and slightly thickened. Blend in vinegar and butter and serve hot over ham.

Chestnut Stuffing for your Christmas Turkey

Gill (mum to Elsie Williams)

ENOUGH FOR A 20LB TURKEY

One of the rituals of Christmas Eve in our home involved all of us sitting round the kitchen table peeling hot chestnuts to make this stuffing. These days you can buy them ready-peeled, but where is the fun in that?! You need approximately 1 1/2 lbs of chestnuts but buy extra as there are always some that are mouldy inside the shells. The exact amounts of chestnuts and sausage meat are not critical.

1 1/2 - 2 LBS CHESTNUTS
1 TURKEY LIVER
1 - 1 1/2 LBS PORK SAUSAGEMEAT
PINCH OF MIXED SPICE
SALT AND PEPPER, TO TASTE
3OZ BUTTER
1 SMALL ONION, FINELY CHOPPED
2 TABLESPOONS BRANDY

Preheat the oven to 160°C/325°F/Gas Mark 3. Make a small knife-cut in the shell of the chestnuts and place them on a baking tray. Bake for approximately 5-10 minutes, then peel with a sharp pointed knife. (As they are more easy to peel when they are warm, you may want to bake them in batches). Place the peeled chestnuts and liver in a food processor and blend. You want the chestnuts to be in small pieces the size of chopped almonds so the stuffing has a bit of crunch.
Add the sausage meat, mixed spice and season.
Fry the chopped onion in the butter and add to the stuffing with the brandy. Use to stuff your turkey and enjoy the rich nutty flavour on Christmas Day. The stuffing will taste just as good cold on Boxing Day too.

the Spring term

CHAPTER TWO

After all that feasting, it's time to restore balance to health and finances, so we open the chapter with some cheap and wholesome meal options. The Spring Term often brings snow, so, in the pages that follow our families from cold northern climes help us ward off the chill with some great one-pot warmers. This is the term when parents are coerced into getting out their whisks for the weekly cake sales.
We have some inspiration to help! Finally, we have some ideas for this term's high days and holidays, and travel to Greece, where they really know how to celebrate Easter!

Cheap and Healthy meals

These recipes, featuring wholesome, frugal ingredients – eggs, lentils and vegetables – are so tasty, even your children will be asking for seconds!

Jamie Oliver's Cauliflower Macaroni

Claire (mum to Luke Dennis)

SERVES 4-6

This recipe, adapted from the one in Jamie Oliver's 30 Minute Meals, is a favourite in our household, as it's quick and easy, but also really, really tasty. It's also different from the usual macaroni cheese and my kids even eat the cauliflower – it's so well disguised!

BY JA

8 RASHERS OF PANCETTA OR STREAKY BACON
1 LARGE HEAD OF CAULIFLOWER
PINCH OF SALT
2 -3 TABLESPOONS OLIVE OIL
500G DRIED MACARONI
250G MATURE CHEDDAR
4 THICK SLICES OF COUNTRY BREAD
A FEW SPRIGS OF ROSEMARY
2 CLOVES OF GARLIC
250G TUB CREME FRAICHE
PARMESAN CHEESE TO SERVE

Preheat the oven to 220°C/425°F/Gas Mark 7. Lay the pancetta or streaky bacon in a roasting tray (approximately 30 x 25cm) and put on the top shelf of the oven. Remove the outer leaves and tough base of the stalk of the cauliflower and cut the head into quarters. Put in a large saucepan, core down, with the pasta. Cover with boiling water, add the salt, drizzle over 2 teaspoons of olive oil and cook according to pasta packet instructions, with the lid on. Grate the cheddar (you can do this more easily in a food processor using a coarse grater attachment). Remove the pancetta or bacon from the oven when crispy, and blitz in a food processor with the bread, rosemary leaves and 1-2 tablespoons of olive oil until you have a coarse breadcrumb consistency (or pound in a pestle and mortar). Put a colander over a bowl then drain the pasta and cauliflower, reserving the pasta water. Tip pasta and cauliflower into the roasting tray that you cooked your pancetta in, and put over a low heat. Add 400ml (or just under a pint) of the reserved pasta water from the bowl. Crush in the 2 unpeeled cloves of garlic and mix in the crème fraîche and grated cheddar, gently breaking up the cauliflower with tongs or a potato masher. Have a taste and correct seasoning. It should be nice and loose; if not, add another splash of pasta water. Spread out evenly and scatter over the breadcrumbs. Put on the top shelf of the oven for about 8 minutes, or until golden and bubbling. Take it to the table and shave over some Parmesan.

Reasons Why to eat Greens

1 There good for you
2 You get a chocolate biscuit
3

Reasons why to NOT eat Greens

1 There the opisit from tasty
2 Your wasting your time
3 They ruin a meal

BY MIA

BY GILBER

Ballymaloe Spicy Lentil Burgers

Francesca (mum to Molly and Louis McKenna)

SERVES 5-10 (MAKES 10 BURGERS)

This gem of a recipe has been adapted from the bible that is Darina Allen's Ballymaloe Cookery Course. It's delicious frugal fare, especially when served with chunky homemade chips and homemade mayonnaise, as the recipe suggests. It's equally good if you're entertaining families and need something that will be devoured by kids and parents, vegetarians and carnivores alike!

2 TABLESPOONS OF OLIVE OIL
1 GARLIC CLOVE, CRUSHED
1 LARGE ONION, FINELY CHOPPED
1 CELERY STICK, FINELY CHOPPED
1 LARGE CARROT, FINELY CHOPPED
225G GREEN LENTILS, BOILED
   FOR 25-30 MINUTES AND DRAINED
1 1/2 TEASPOONS GROUND CUMIN
2 TEASPOONS GROUND CORIANDER
6 TABLESPOONS PARSLEY, CHOPPED
1 TABLESPOON LEMON JUICE
SALT AND FRESHLY GROUND PEPPER
1 EGG, BEATEN
50G WHITE BREADCRUMBS
WHITE SEASONED FLOUR
OIL FOR SHALLOW FRYING

Heat the olive oil in a frying pan then sauté the garlic, onion, carrot and celery for 10-12 minutes over a medium heat until softened and lightly browned. Add the lentils, spices, parsley, lemon juice and seasoning. Cook for 5 minutes, then blend (using a food processor or hand blender) with the egg and breadcrumbs until the mixture holds together, but still has a course texture. Transfer to a mixing bowl. Cover a baking tray with greaseproof paper. With wet hands, shape the mixture into 8 burgers and dip in seasoned flour. Place them on the baking sheet, cover and chill for 30 minutes. Heat the oil in a frying pan. Cook the burgers in batches for 5-7 minutes on each side. Pat with kitchen paper, in order to remove excess oil. Serve with Raita (see page 39) or homemade mayonnaise mixed with a little roasted and ground coriander.

Pastry-less Quiche Lorraine

Karine (mum to Allia and Pablo Sleiman-Genevee)

SERVES 2 ADULTS
OR 3-4 CHILDREN

3 EGGS
1/2L MILK
100G PLAIN FLOUR
100G CHEESE, GRATED
SALT AND PEPPER (TO TASTE)
FILLINGS, EG COOKED
   GREENS, SUCH AS CHOPPED
   SPINACH, FRIED MUSHROOMS,
   TINNED TUNA, HAM

My French mum used to cook this dish when I was a child and I used to (and still do) love it! Now I cook it for my children. It's a great dish for hiding greens, such as cooked spinach or broccoli, as it's so tasty.

Preheat the oven to 220°C/425°F/Gas Mark 7. Mix together the eggs, milk, flour, salt and pepper (this is easier with an electric mixer). Pour the mix into a round quiche tin or equivalent. Then add the grated cheese and any other fillings. (We like two tins of tuna in brine along with cooked green vegetables.) Cook in the oven for about 40 minutes, or until a skewer inserted into the middle comes out clean.

Child-friendly Omelette

Munna (mum to Maryam and Sophia Rafique)

SERVES 1

I have 4 girls. They all love cooking and baking and 'helping out in the kitchen'. This is not an easy task for me! However, this omelette recipe keeps us all happy, as it is simple and healthy, and the girls enjoy choosing their favourite fillings.

1 TABLESPOON OLIVE OIL OR
  BUTTER
FOR FRYING
1 SMALL SHALLOT/HALF A RED
  ONION, DICED
2 FREE-RANGE EGGS
2-3 TABLESPOONS FULL
  CREAM MILK
PINCH OF SALT

FILLINGS, E.G.
1 GREEN CHILLI, SLICED
1/2 RED PEPPER, DICED
SMALL CHUNK OF LEEK, SLICED
OLIVES, CHOPPED
FRESH CORIANDER, CHOPPED

Soften the onions in the olive oil or butter. Add the red pepper and salt and fry until soft. Add the chilli and leeks if you wish (my eldest daughter Aisha loves to add these for the colour!) and continue frying for another minute or two until onions are golden-brown and all the vegetables are soft. Beat the eggs in a bowl, add the milk and pour over the other ingredients. When the egg has almost solidified (after a minute or two) add the coriander and olives, if using, cook for another minute then flip to ensure both sides are cooked. Serve with a warm baguette or a side salad.

MY MUM'S A REALLY GOOD COOK BECAUSE SHE COOKS EVERYTHING WITH LOVE.
Kyane Perera

Sri Lankan Lentil Curry with Spinach

Rushni (mum to Kyane Perera)

SERVES 2-3

Coconut milk is a typical Sri Lankan ingredient, and elevates this humble collection of ingredients into a really tasty main meal. We eat this healthy dish often in our house, with rice or some type of flat bread. Don't be worried if your children aren't used to spices - they will soon acquire a taste, just like my son Kyane has!

250G RED LENTILS
1 LARGE ONION, FINELY SLICED
1 TOMATO, CHOPPED
5-7 CURRY LEAVES
1 GREEN CHILLI, SLICED (OPTIONAL)
1/2 TEASPOON MILD CHILLI POWDER
  (TRUST ME, THIS IS HARDLY
  NOTICEABLE)
1/2 TEASPOON TURMERIC
200G BABY LEAF SPINACH
250ML COCONUT MILK (MADE FROM
  DRY COCONUT MILK POWDER, OR YOU
  CAN USE COCONUT MILK FROM A TIN)
SALT (TO TASTE)

Wash the lentils well and place in a wide open pan such as a wok, along with the onion, tomato, curry leaves, green chilli, chilli powder and turmeric.
Add enough water to just cover, and simmer on a medium heat, stirring from time to time so that the lentils don't stick to the bottom of the pan.
After 5 minutes add the coconut milk and keep stirring for 10-15 minutes, until the lentils are cooked and tender.
Add the spinach and stir to wilt, then season with salt, to taste.

Moosewood West African Groundnut Stew

Cadence (mum to Zaviana and Satya Lane)

SERVES 6

This recipe, adapted from my hands-down favourite cookbook, Moosewood, is a firm favourite in our family. Even my very fussy 3-year-old - who barely touches most vegetables - gobbles it up! He loves the okra, as they look like flowers when sliced - excellent as they are so good for you! Serve with rice and any of the following: hard-boiled eggs; chopped spring onions, fresh parsley or coriander; cubed papaya; sliced bananas, mangoes, pineapples or oranges; grated coconut; whole or crushed peanuts.

BY ANIA & SOFIA

    2 LARGE ONIONS
    2 TABLESPOONS GROUNDNUT OR VEGETABLE OIL
    1/2 TEASPOON CAYENNE PEPPER OR OTHER GROUND DRIED CHILLIS
    (I USUALLY ONLY PUT IN A TINY PINCH)
    1 TEASPOON CRUSHED GARLIC (I USE ABOUT 5 OR 6 CLOVES)
    2 CUPS CHOPPED RED OR GREEN CABBAGE
    3 CUPS CUBED SWEET POTATOES
    3 CUPS TOMATO JUICE
    1 CUP APPLE OR APRICOT JUICE (ALTHOUGH ANY JUICE WORKS)
    1 TEASPOON SALT
    1 TEASPOON GRATED. PEELED FRESH GINGER (I USUALLY
      DO ABOUT 1 OR 2 TABLESPOONS!)
    1 TABLESPOON CHOPPED FRESH CORIANDER (OPTIONAL)
    2 TOMATOES. CHOPPED
    1 1/2 - 2 CUPS CHOPPED OKRA
    1/2 CUP PEANUT BUTTER

Soften the onions in the oil for about 10 minutes then stir in the cayenne pepper and garlic and sauté for a couple more minutes. Add the cabbage and the sweet potatoes, cover and heat for a few minutes. Mix in the juices, salt, ginger, coriander and tomatoes. Cover and simmer for about 15 minutes, until the sweet potatoes are tender. Add the okra and simmer for 5 more minutes. Stir in the nut butter and simmer for a few more minutes. Add more juice or water if the stew is too thick.

Sage and Onion Stuffing

Victoria Head

frugal tip: serve some tasty stuffing with your roast to make a small amount of meat stretch further!

SERVES 3-4 PEOPLE (UNLESS ONE IS MY BIG SISTER. WHO WILL EAT HALF!)

This is my Dad's recipe, which we make when we have roast chicken for Sunday lunch. We cook it in a separate dish, so that it gets nice and crispy.

Peel and chop a large onion and add to a lightly oiled frying pan on a medium heat. When the onion is soft and starting to brown, add 1 crushed garlic clove, give a quick stir, then remove from the heat. Meanwhile, break two slices of bread into thumbnail sized pieces and place in a bowl with 1 lightly beaten egg, 2 heaped teaspoons of dried sage and a sprinkling of salt and pepper. Stir gently until all ingredients are coated in the egg, then mix in the fried onions and garlic. Tip into a small, oiled ovenproof dish and cook for 25-30 mins at 180°C/350°F/Gas Mark 4, or until the top of the stuffing is becoming crisp. Check the stuffing after 15 minutes and drizzle over a spoonful of olive oil or some of the meat juices if it starts to look too dry.

Linsen und Spätzle mit Saitenwürstchen (Swabian Lentil Stew with Frankfurters)

The Ludwig Family (Leah, Hannah and Jacob)

SERVES 4

This is a traditional southwest German dish from Swabia (a region around Stuttgart), originating from the times when meat was hard to come by. Lentils were one of the only things to grow on the poor soil, and, with their high protein content, made a fantastic substitution for meat. Nowadays it's traditional to add saitenwürstchen (unsmoked frankfurters). It is a big favourite with children, but no Swabian's week would be complete without this meal: some even refer to it as 'the Swabian's heaven'!

30G BUTTER
50G FLOUR
1-2 ONIONS (150G)
500ML VEGETABLE STOCK
3 CANS GREEN LENTILS (OR 250G
    DRIED, COOKED UNTIL SOFT)
SALT (TO TASTE)
2 PEPPERCORNS
1 CLOVE
2 TABLESPOONS RED WINE VINEGAR
PIECE OF SPECK OR BACON (OPTIONAL)
12-16 SAITENWÜRSTCHEN
    (SUPERMARKET VACUUM-PACKED
    FRANKFURTERS CAN BE USED)

Melt the butter and mix with the flour to make a roux; add the onions and fry until soft. Gradually whisk in the stock. Drain the lentils and add to the broth. Season with salt, peppercorns, clove and vinegar, and simmer for approximately 20 minutes. At this stage you could add a piece of speck or bacon to make the dish more hearty. Add the frankfurters and let them simmer in the broth for a few more minutes. Don't let it boil or the sausages will pop open. Serve with spätzle (see below) and an extra helping of vinegar, if liked.

Spätzle (Swabian Noodles)

Laura (mum to Freddie and Theo Pflanz)

SERVES 4-5

Spätzle (spaetzle) means 'little sparrow' in German. They are a bit like pasta, and usually cooked in boiling water then pan fried in butter. They come from southern Germany (originally Swabia), but are now also popular in the Black Forest. You can serve them as a side dish, or melt grated cheese on them. Freddie and Theo have them for just about every meal when we are on holiday in Germany.

500G PLAIN FLOUR
5 EGGS
ABOUT 175ML WATER
    (YOU CAN ALSO
    USE MILK)
1 TEASPOON SALT

Sift the flour and salt into a bowl. In another bowl whisk the eggs and water (or milk) together. Make a well in the flour, pour in the egg mixture and stir with a wooden spoon until you have a dough that is elastic and bubbly. Bring a large pan of salted water to the boil. Hold a large-holed colander over the pan and push the spätzle dough through the holes with a spoon or spatula into the boiling water (or cut into small pieces on a chopping board and drop into the water by hand). Boil for about 4 minutes or until the spätzle rise to the top of the pan. (It is easier to do this in batches.) You can drain the spätzle and serve them with some melted butter, but it's even nicer to fry them in butter for a few minutes until they start to go golden.

It's cold...its dark... we have colds! Chicken soup is the answer!

winter Soul Food

BY JASMIN

Oma's Chicken Soup

Sarah (mum to William Mallon)

SERVES 4

Our children's Dutch grandmother swears by this chicken soup to ward off coughs and colds!
She and their Grandpa are very healthy eaters.

1 WHOLE CHICKEN
   (FREE-RANGE OR ORGANIC)
1 CARROT
1 CELERY STICK
1 CLOVE OF GARLIC
1/2 ONION
ANY OTHER VEG YOU WOULD
   LIKE TO PUT IN
1 VEGETABLE STOCK CUBE

Put the whole lot in a big pot of water and simmer for one hour or till the meat falls of the bones. Take carcass out of the stock and shred the chicken meat. Throw away the bones and skin and add chicken bits to the stock. Ready to serve.

Or try these...

Chicken and Lentil Soup

Sebastian (dad to Louis Motte)

SERVES 4-5

This recipe, adapted from one in my well-used Cordon Bleu cookbook, always reminds me of my French grandma, Mamie Jeanne. What child likes soup? Not many, and I was one of them, until one day when I was about 6, Mamie Jeanne gave me a bowl of hers. It is one of the few meals in my life that I still remember trying for the first time, like my first McDonald's cheeseburger in 1990 (it took a long time for McDonald's to reach Lille!). What was her secret? Heston Blumenthal opened my eyes years later whilst I was reading his Heston at Home cookbook: Mamie knew exactly how much salt to put in. She seasoned it to the point where, with just one more pinch, the soup would have been spoiled — a quantity that I never dared to use before and now only do in my bowl of soup. The other secret is to always soften the vegetables in oil before adding the water. This creates an explosion of flavours and makes the soup one of the most delicious meals on a cold winter evening. Oh que c'est bon!

2 TABLESPOONS OLIVE OIL
1 ONION, CHOPPED
100G BACON, CUT INTO SMALL PIECES
1 STALK OF CELERY, CHOPPED
4 CARROTS, CHOPPED
1 BOUQUET GARNI (THYME, PARSLEY, BAY LEAF)
LEFTOVER ROAST CHICKEN CARCASS, SKIN
    REMOVED (FOR STOCK - REMOVE THE BREAST
    MEAT IF STILL SOME LEFT ON THE CHICKEN)
3LITRES WATER
300G PUY LENTILS
4 CHICKEN BREASTS, CUBED OR CUT INTO
    STRIPS (OPTIONAL DEPENDING ON THE
    AMOUNT OF MEAT LEFT FROM THE ROAST)
PARSLEY, CHOPPED (TO GARNISH)
SALT AND PEPPER TO TASTE (SEE ABOVE!)

Heat the olive oil in a large pan. Add the onion and bacon and fry gently until the onion is soft. Add the vegetables and herbs and cook for 5 minutes. Add the chicken carcass, 3 litres of water and the lentils and bring to the boil, then reduce heat and simmer for 1 hour, stirring several times. Meanwhile, stir-fry the chicken breasts, if extra is needed, and put aside. After 1 hour, remove the leftover chicken bones from the pan and cook for a further 15 minutes, then remove herbs and whizz in a blender until smooth. Season to taste. Add the chicken breast meat to the soup, heat through until piping hot and serve with a garnish of fresh parsley.

Leek and Potato Soup

Emma (mum to Jack Hardy)

SERVES 4-6

My grandfather had a large allotment and grew lots of what we ate as kids. This recipe came from my grandma, who would create a big pan for the whole family. We make this soup often during winter as it's such an easy one to make. Frankie can make it herself now and even Jack doesn't need much help.

4 LARGE LEEKS
2 MEDIUM POTATOES, PEELED
AND DICED
1 MEDIUM ONION, CHOPPED SMALL
50G BUTTER
850ML STOCK - CAN BE
    VEGETABLE OR CHICKEN
275ML MILK
SALT AND PEPPER TO SEASON

Top and tail the leeks, split down the middle and slice finely. Wash thoroughly to ensure the leeks are free from soil between the layers. In a large, thick-bottomed saucepan, melt the butter on a gentle heat and add the leeks, potato and onion. Stir well with a wooden spoon, season with salt and pepper, cover and sweat on a low heat for around 15 minutes until onion is soft. Then add the stock and milk and simmer gently, to avoid the milk curdling, until all the vegetables are tender. Take off the heat and purée in the pan with a blender. Add a swirl of cream and a snip of chives to serve. Best with warm, crusty bread.

Ukrainian Borsch

Roman (dad to Marco Van Papendorp-Honcharuk)

SERVES 8-10

Borsch, a hearty vegetable soup popular in many eastern and central European countries, is the national dish and, indeed, national symbol of the Ukraine. Whilst each country has its own version – up to 40 different ingredients can find their way into a good plate of borsch – the one common ingredient is beetroot, which gives the dish its characteristic red colour and in fact its name ('br'sch'

a sprinkling of fresh dill

a dollop of sour cream

is the old Slavic word for 'beet'). Hot borsch (typically made with beef or pork broth and starchy vegetables) can be eaten as a starter with dark rye bread, however, being so hearty and nourishing is often served as a one-course meal. It can be enjoyed throughout the year, but there is nothing better than sitting down to a big bowl of steaming hot borsch when you come in on a cold day. It will warm your body and soul, bringing much more optimism to your life's challenges.

It is often said that there are as many different kinds of borsch as there are cooks in the Ukraine. The below recipe is a good starting point should you wish to carry on the tradition of creating your own version. Feel free to experiment, for example, replace meat with dried beans if you are a vegetarian; leave out the garlic if you have a business meeting the next day! There is only one rule to stick to: a good Ukrainian borsch should be thick with vegetables. According to tradition, a wooden spoon should stand upright when stuck into the pot! If you make a big pot any leftovers can be frozen, but borsch keeps well in the fridge for up to a week and is even more delicious served the next day! (NB reheat to boiling point before serving).

note from some other beetroot aficionados:

1.5 - 2LBS BEEF ON THE BONE,
EG CHUCK, SHIN, OXTAIL
(OR PORK ON THE BONE)
3.5L WATER
2-3 BAY LEAVES
6 BLACK PEPPERCORNS
SUNFLOWER OIL
1 MEDIUM BEETROOT, ABOUT
300G, PEELED AND CUT INTO
SHORT, THIN STRIPS ABOUT
4MM THICK (USE RUBBER
GLOVES IF YOU DON'T WANT
RED HANDS!)
1 TEASPOON VINEGAR (EG RED
OR WHITE WINE VINEGAR)
3 MEDIUM CARROTS, DICED
2 MEDIUM ONIONS, FINELY
CHOPPED
2 STEMS PARSLEY, CHOPPED
1/2 MEDIUM WHITE CABBAGE,
FINELY SLICED
5 MEDIUM POTATOES, DICED
2-3 TABLESPOONS TOMATO PUREE
BUNCH OF DILL, LEAVES AND
STEMS, CHOPPED
3-5 CLOVES GARLIC, ROUGHLY
CHOPPED
SALT AND SUGAR, TO TASTE

TO SERVE:
SOUR CREAM, 1-2 TABLESPOONS
PER PERSON
EXTRA CHOPPED DILL,
1-2 TEASPOONS PER PERSON

Place meat, water, salt, peppercorns and bay leaves in a large cooking pot. Bring to the boil, skimming frequently to remove fat and foam. Reduce heat and simmer, uncovered, until meat is tender, about 1.5-2 hours. Strain the beef stock into large saucepan and set aside. Take the meat from the bones; shred and set aside (discard bones). While the meat is cooking, fry the beetroot in a little sunflower oil until just tender, then add vinegar (this preserves the colour). Remove from the pan and set aside. Wipe out pan and add some more oil, then fry carrots, onions and parsley, until the onion starts to turn golden.

"IN OUR HOUSEHOLD, RUSSIAN BORSCHT IS A WINTER STAPLE AS A LIGHT DINNER OR STARTER. ALTHOUGH IT TAKES A WHILE TO COOK, IT'S NOT DIFFICULT TO MAKE AND ALLOWS THE OPPORTUNITY FOR THE CHEF TO SHOO THE REST OF THE FAMILY OUT OF THE KITCHEN AND TUNE THE INTERNET RADIO TO THE BBC RUSSIAN SERVICE IN PEACE. AS A NOTE TO ANYONE AIMING TO SERVE BORSCHT IT MAY HELP TO KNOW THAT BEETROOT STAINS DISAPPEAR QUITE EASILY FROM CLOTHES WHEN YOU POUR HOT WATER ONTO THE STAIN BEFORE PUTTING THE ITEM INTO THE WASH!"

Antoinette (mum to Nikolai and Sophia Harin)

Add the bay leaves and potatoes to the reserved beef stock. Simmer for 10 minutes then add the sautéed carrots, onions, parsley and beetroot, along with the cabbage and tomato puree. Stir well then simmer for 10-20 minutes, until all the vegetables are tender. Add salt and pepper to taste, along with a small amount of sugar if necessary. Add the reserved meat to the pot. Grind the garlic and dill with a pestle and mortar and add to the pot. Leave to stand for 10 minutes. To serve in true Ukrainian fashion top with a sprinkle of dill and a dollop of sour cream – and enjoy one of the Ukraine's wonderful gifts to humanity!

"IN POLAND WE EAT OUR BORSCHT BRIGHT PINK WITH ALL VEGETABLES STRAINED AND REMOVED, AND SERVE WITH SMALL DUMPLINGS CALLED 'LITTLE EARS'"

Basia (mum to Sofia, Ania and Derik Vercueil)

Spanish Lentil Soup with Chorizo

Ana (mum to Daniel, Naomi and Noah Bronk-Navas)

SERVES 4-5

More than just a soup, this is a meal in itself and a great winter warmer. My mum sent me off to university in England with this recipe, recommending I always cook a huge pot and freeze spare portions. Well, chorizo was hard to find in London 20 years ago. I made do with bacon, which can't have been too bad, as there was never anything left over to freeze once my friends were gone! Happily chorizo is now available everywhere. I use the mild version when cooking this for my children.

HALF A RING OF CHORIZO (SPICY
   OR MILD), SLICED
250G GREEN LENTILS (MORE OR LESS)
1 ONION, CHOPPED
2 CLOVES GARLIC, FINELY CHOPPED
1 RED PEPPER AND/OR COURGETTE,
   CHOPPED
A FEW POTATOES, PEELED
EXTRA VIRGIN OLIVE OIL, FOR
   FRYING

In a big pot, fry the onions, garlic, red pepper / courgette and chorizo in extra virgin olive oil. Cover until all vegetables take a reddish colour from frying with the chorizo. Pour in the lentils with plenty of water and cover. Simmer for 20-30 minutes, stirring and adding water as necessary. In a separate pot, cook the potatoes, adding them to the lentil soup just before it's ready. My daughter does not like potatoes much so I often serve this with crusty bread instead.

Chupe (Peruvian Soup)

Heejin (mum to Samuel Romero)

SERVES 4 TO 5

This soup is quick and easy to prepare, nutritious and totally delicious! My husband is Peruvian and whenever I visit my mother-in-law we are treated to an array of Peruvian dishes. One of his absolute favourites is this simple dish 'chupe', which reminds him of his childhood. This particular recipe uses no oil, which is my mother-in-law's own way of preparing it, and so is extremely healthy! I recommend this recipe to mums and dads who are feeling too tired to prepare something too complicated. This will fill your family's tummies. I hope you enjoy it!

300G RUMP STEAK OR FREE RANGE
   CHICKEN BREAST FILLET
3 MEDIUM-SIZED RED POTATOES,
   PEELED AND CHOPPED
1 CARROT, CHOPPED
1 LEEK, SLICED
1 RED CHILLI (WHOLE)
1 TEASPOON CHILLI POWDER
1/2 TEASPOON GARLIC POWDER
1 TEASPOON GROUND CUMIN
1 CUBE CHICKEN STOCK
SALT AND BLACK PEPPER (TO TASTE)
1 SMALL HANDFUL OF SPAGHETTI
1 SMALL BUNCH OF CORIANDER,
   CHOPPED

Chop the vegetables and meat into bite-size pieces. Put the potatoes, carrot and leek into a large pot of water and bring to the boil for approximately 10 minutes. Add the chicken stock and seasoning followed by the beef or chicken pieces.
Put in the whole red chilli and snap the spaghetti into the pot and boil until everything is cooked through. Add some chopped coriander towards the end and simmer for the last 3 minutes. Serve immediately with warm pitta bread.

 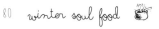

Beef Stroganoff

Irina (mum to Nicole Williams)

SERVES 4

I've lived in many different countries over the years, so I like to bring different cuisines and tastes to the table: Asian food (using spices from Georgia); German sauerkraut with smoked sausages; salmon marinated in salt, Swedish style; light Californian salads. But on a cold day I yearn for Beef Stroganoff and the earthy smell of buckwheat. My memories are of the whole family sitting together at the table in Russia, looking out of the window at the glistening snow and enjoying this warming dish, with obligatory sour cream and a slice of pickled cucumber. It's such a satisfying dish, yet is so easy, and only takes 30 minutes to make.

3 TABLESPOONS OLIVE OIL
600G BEEF FILLET, CUT INTO SMALL STRIPS
30G UNSALTED BUTTER
3 LARGE SHALLOTS, FINELY CHOPPED
1 TABLESPOON PAPRIKA
50G MUSHROOMS, THINLY SLICED
25ML WHITE WINE VINEGAR
50ML BRANDY
250ML CHICKEN STOCK
200ML SOUR CREAM

Heat the oil in a frying pan over a high heat until very hot. Add the meat and fry in batches for 3-5 minutes, stirring occasionally, until lightly browned. Remove from the pan, set aside and keep warm. Melt the butter in the pan, add the shallots and cook for 2 minutes or until soft but not coloured. Add the paprika and stir for around a minute, then add the mushrooms and cook over a high heat until all the liquid has evaporated. Add the brandy, cook until the liquid is reduced to half, then add the stock and reduce to half again. Finally, add half of the sour cream and return the meat to the pan to reheat. Serve with buckwheat or rice, and the remaining sour cream on the side.

Scottish Stovies

Laura (mum to Magnus and Howard Folland)

SERVES 3-4

This is one of those age-old thrifty, very simple, dishes based on using leftovers from a Sunday roast, and truly heartwarming when the temperature is freezing, as it often is in Scotland! Each family has their own recipe – this is my mum's version, passed down to her from my great-grandmother, with whom she lived during the blitz in 1941. Lorne is flat square sausage (hard to find outside Scotland, although my local butcher will make it up for me if I pre-order). The general consensus seems to be that it should be served with oatcakes and beetroots (although we never have!). My kids moan 'not again' when I serve stovies (as I used to do) but they always finish what's on their plates and I still ask my mum to make it every time I visit her.

1 TABLESPOON OIL
1 ONION, DICED
4 SLICES LORNE, CUT INTO 4 PIECES (OR SUBSTITUTE
  WITH REGULAR SAUSAGES, MINCE, DICED MEAT OR CUBES
  OF CORNED BEEF)
3 CARROTS, SLICED
3 LARGE POTATOES, PEELED AND THICKLY SLICED
1/2 SMALL SWEDE, CUBED (OPTIONAL)
400ML BEEF STOCK
SPLASH WORCESTERSHIRE SAUCE, TO TASTE (OPTIONAL)
SALT AND PEPPER, TO TASTE

NOT AGAIN!!!

Soften the onion in the oil in a large pot. Brown the sausage in a frying pan to add flavour and eliminate some of the fat, then add to the onion along with the rest of the ingredients. Bring to the boil then simmer gently for at least an hour until the vegetables are soft (or leave to cook on a low setting in the slow cooker if out for the day).

"MY KIDS MOAN "NOT AGAIN" WHEN I SERVE STOVIES - AS I USED TO DO - BUT THEY ALWAYS FINISH WHAT'S ON THEIR PLATES."

Laura King

Irish Stew

Niamh (mum to Andrew O'Connor)

SERVES 4-6 PEOPLE

This was a family favourite growing up in Dublin – my mother's version of a traditional Irish recipe. As children we would mash all of the vegetables into the potato (as we did not want to taste them separately) and pour the broth on top. I now do this for Andrew and my two daughters – one of the easiest ways to ensure they eat their vegetables. It has become a favourite in our family too.

1-1.5KG BONELESS LAMB
    SHOULDER, CUT INTO
    BITE-SIZE CHUNKS (ASK
    YOUR BUTCHER TO DO THIS
    FOR YOU)
2 SPRIGS ROSEMARY
1 ONION, FINELY CHOPPED
3 CARROTS, CHOPPED
1 LEEK, CHOPPED
1 PARSNIP, CHOPPED
0.5 SMALL TURNIP, CHOPPED
3 MEDIUM POTATOES, PEELED
    AND BROKEN INTO CHUNKS
SALT AND PEPPER TO TASTE
CHOPPED PARSLEY,
    TO GARNISH

Put the meat, herbs and vegetables into a slow cooker or large pot and cover with water. Simmer all day (ideal if you are going to work) in a slow cooker or for 2 hours in large pot. Remove the rosemary before serving and add chopped parsley. Serve with mashed potatoes or wheaten bread (see recipe below).

Wheaten Bread (Wholemeal Soda Bread)

Niamh (mum to Andrew O'Connor)

MAKES 1 MEDIUM-SIZE LOAF

This was my granny's recipe, which I have had to amend as I find it difficult to get the original ingredients in London. However, it is still very similar to the bread my granny and mother cooked for us growing up. Rather than providing precise measurements of ingredients, you need to apply your own judgement regarding consistency and

texture of the dough. This is one of the most versatile bread recipes. It takes only an hour from start to finish. I add flaxseed in winter and olives or sun-dried tomatoes during the summer.

1 PINT MILK
PINCH OF SALT
1 TEASPOON
BICARBONATE OF SODA
APPROXIMATELY 550G
    WHOLEMEAL FLOUR

Preheat the oven to 140°C/275°F/Gas Mark 1. Lightly grease a large loaf tin. Pour the milk into a mixing bowl. Add the salt, bicarbonate of soda and a little wholemeal flour and stir. Keep adding the flour slowly until the mixture forms a ball of dough. Flour the counter surface and knead the dough for 30-40 seconds. Shape to fit your bread tin. Place in the oven and cook for approximately 30-40 minutes. To check that the bread is fully cooked, I find it best to use a skewer, which should come out clean. In addition, you can check by tapping on the underside, which should sound hollow. Finally after removing the bread from the oven and bread tin, wrap in a tea towel and leave to cool.

Guinness Brown Bread

Marie (mum to Oliver and Isabel Monger)

MAKES 1 LOAF

This is my mum's recipe. It's delicious, especially with soups and stews.

450G COARSE WHOLEMEAL FLOUR
2 LEVEL TEASPOONS
   BICARBONATE OF SODA
25G PINHEAD OATS
4 TABLESPOONS DEMERARA SUGAR
100G CHOPPED WALNUTS
   (OPTIONAL)
50G BUTTER
1 TABLESPOON TREACLE
400 ML GUINNESS
   (CAN OR BOTTLE)

Preheat the oven to 190°C/375°F/Gas Mark 5. Lightly grease a 900g loaf tin. Put the butter and treacle into a saucepan on a low heat and allow to slowly melt. Put the flour, oats, sugar and chopped nuts (if used) into a bowl, sieve in the bicarbonate of soda and mix well. When the butter has melted, add the Guinness and stir.
Add the liquid ingredients to the dry, and mix well. Transfer the mixture to the prepared tin and bake for 40-50 minutes or until risen and when tapped underneath makes a hollow sound. Wrap in a clean tea towel and allow to cool. You should wait 1 day before cutting.

Braised Spiced Red Cabbage

Simon from Riverford Organic Farms (dad to Alex Harrop)

SERVES 4

This recipe, taken from the Riverford Organic Farms website (www.riverford.co.uk), has all the appeal of classic spiced red cabbage, but takes less than an hour to make rather than the usual three or four.

1 RED CABBAGE, FINELY
   SHREDDED
2 COOKING APPLES, PEELED,
   CORED AND CHOPPED
1 ONION, CHOPPED
SLUG SUNFLOWER OIL
AROUND 5 ALLSPICE BERRIES,
   ROUGHLY CRUSHED, IF YOU
   CAN FIND THEM - OTHERWISE
   LEAVE OUT
2 CLOVES
1 STICK CINNAMON
1 BAY LEAF
1 1/2 TABLESPOONS DARK
   SOFT BROWN SUGAR
1 1/2 TABLESPOONS CIDER
   OR RED WINE VINEGAR

Sweat spices, onions and apple in the oil in a large heavy-based pan until beginning to soften. Add the bay leaf and cabbage and enough water to come about half way up the cabbage. Cover and turn up heat so cabbage is boiling, return to simmer and cook for 30-40 minutes until cabbage is tender. By now the liquid should have reduced to about an inch in the bottom of the pan but if there is too much water left, uncover the pan and boil vigorously to reduce it further. Add in the vinegar, sugar and seasoning, taste and adjust so that you have a good balance of sweet and sour. Serve straight away or cool and reheat later. This dish also freezes very well.

Pickled Cucumber

Jenny (mum to Maya and Lily Buchanan)

SERVES 4-6

A recipe from my Swedish mother, which I use when I'm not sure what else to add as a side dish to a meal or just need an extra 'something' to add to the table. This takes very little time and effort, is delicious with rich meat dishes and always goes down well at barbecues.

1 WHOLE CUCUMBER
2 TABLESPOONS WATER
2 TABLESPOONS CLEAR
   PICKLING VINEGAR
1 TABLESPOON SUGAR
PINCH OF BLACK PEPPER
   PARSLEY OR DILL
   TO YOUR TASTE

Peel the cucumber and, using a cheese slice or mandolin, slice into wafer thin rounds. Put the cucumber into a bowl and add the water, pickling vinegar and the sugar. Give it a stir and add the pinch of black pepper and parsley or dill to your taste. This can be served straight away as the cucumber quickly absorbs the taste but can also be kept in the fridge for a few days.

... and something nice for afterwards

Lemon Surprise Pudding

Adam (dad to Oliver and Matthew Richford)

SERVES 4

My mum was an avid collector of recipes. Over the years she pasted them into a scrapbook, which Dad later arranged to have bound with an enduring hard cover. Many of our favourite recipes, including this one, featured in the book of Richford Family Recipes, which mum gave all us kids when we left home. Lemon Surprise Pudding was Dad's favourite dessert to have after the Sunday roast and was popular with us all, due to the fact that it didn't have rhubarb hidden in it (unlike many of mum's pies and crumbles!). The 'surprise' is that it's very wet going into the oven but comes out sponge-like, with a creamy lemon sauce hidden underneath.

2 OZ BUTTER
2 EGGS
JUST UNDER HALF A PINT
   OF MILK
3 1/2 OZ CASTER SUGAR
2 OZ SELF-RAISING FLOUR,
   SIFTED
1 LARGE LEMON

Preheat the oven to 180°C/350°F/Gas Mark 4. Lightly grease an ovenproof dish (we always used a ceramic soufflé dish, approximately 8in in diameter). Grate rind and squeeze juice of lemon. Separate eggs and beat whites stiffly. Cream butter with grated rind of lemon and sugar. When, fluffy beat in the egg yolks then stir in the milk. Next add the lemon juice and fold in the egg whites lightly but thoroughly with a metal spoon. Bake for about 45 minutes till pudding is golden brown. Delicious served with cream.

BY SOFIA

the School Cake sale!

Cupcakes 20p

Rocky Road 30p

bu...

It's a few weeks into the new year. All is quiet, as the new term's rhythm gently beds in. And then the terrifying sound comes, striking fear into the hearts of mothers still recovering from Christmas. It's the heavy machinery of the PTA rolling over into the new term and cranking up a gear. Let the Friday morning cake sales commence!

cheeseburger cakes 30p

Brownies 30p

This recipe was passed on to me by my grandmother, Bertha Alice Bodger. She was an extraordinary woman, who ran a hotel in Guernsey and managed to provide full-board catering on post-war rations.

Like her I have done my fair share of catering, and must have baked around 10,000 of these cakes over the years for weddings, christenings, school fairs and various farmers markets around South West London, where they developed quite a fan base, with customers including Jerry Hall and Rob Brydon. I am always asked for the recipe, so here it is.

Elaine's Cupcakes

Elaine (mum to James Harper-Jones)

MAKES 24

CAKES:
250G SALTED BUTTER,
  SOFTENED
250G CASTER SUGAR
250G SELF-RAISING FLOUR
1 TEASPOON BAKING POWDER
1 TEASPOON VANILLA EXTRACT
2 TABLESPOONS MILK
  (APPROXIMATELY)
4 EGGS (WHATEVER YOU HAVE
  IN YOUR FRIDGE)

BUTTERCREAM ICING:
150G SALTED BUTTER,
  SOFTENED
300 ICING SUGAR
1 TEASPOON VANILLA EXTRACT
  OR VANILLA BEAN PASTE
1 TABLESPOON MILK

Preheat the oven to 180°C/350°F/Gas Mark 4. Line two muffin tins with paper cases. Cream the butter and sugar until light and fluffy. (Bertha would have used her wooden spoon and a large dose of elbow grease, but I do this in my freestanding mixer, mixing for a good 10 minutes until the sugar has dissolved.) Gradually add the eggs. (It's not the end of the world if the mixture curdles, but if it does adding a tablespoon of flour will remedy the situation.) Sift the flour and baking powder together, then add it to the wet ingredients and stir until just incorporated, taking care not to over-mix. Add the vanilla extract then enough milk to give a soft batter with a dropping consistency. Fill the cases – I use an ice-cream scoop, which gives just the right amount. Bake for about 20 minutes and remove each cake from the tin to cool on a wire rack (this prevents shrinkage).

For the buttercream icing, whip the butter, vanilla, milk and icing sugar for a good 5-10 minutes until the icing has doubled in volume. (You can use a fork but it's much easier with an electric mixer!) Spoon icing into a piping bag and top the cupcakes once cooled (a little practise may be required but you'll soon get the knack!). I use a large star nozzle (size 5). Decorate as desired.

Rocky Road

Jane (mum to Henry Turrell and Martha Upward)

MAKES APPROXIMATELY 24 SQUARES

This is an amalgamation of a number of Rocky Road recipes. We often give them as little gifts; grandads love them too! I vary the filling, sometimes adding crunchy nut cornflakes, or dark chilli chocolate for a grown-up version. Popping candy sprinkled on top is also fun!

125G UNSALTED BUTTER, SOFTENED
200G PLAIN CHOCOLATE DIGESTIVES
300G GOOD QUALITY DARK
   CHOCOLATE, BROKEN INTO PIECES
125G GOLDEN SYRUP
4 SMALL MERINGUE NESTS
   (ABOUT 30G)
40G MINI MARSHMALLOWS
SPRINKLING ICING SUGAR, TO DUST

Lightly grease a 24cm (9in) square baking tin. Gently heat the butter, chocolate and golden syrup in a heavy-bottomed sauce-pan until melted, adding some of the marshmallows towards the end. Remove from the heat. Whizz the digestives in a food processor (or smash them in a plastic bag with a rolling pin) until there is a mix of chunks and crumbs. Put the crushed bis-cuits into a mixing bowl and crumble in the meringue nests and marshmallows. Fold about two thirds of the melted chocolate into the biscuit mix then tip into the baking tin, pushing the mix into the corners. Pour over the remaining melted chocolate mixture, cover with cling film and pop in the fridge overnight or for a few hours. To serve, cut into squares and dust with icing sugar.

Baked Lollipops

Kerstin (mum to Leah, Hannah and Jacob Ludwig)

MAKES 15

This recipe, from a German cookery magazine, is one the girls beg me to make whenever there is a cake sale at school. They are always a big hit in the playground!

CAKES:
15 ICE LOLLY STICKS
120G BUTTER, SOFTENED
120G SUGAR
1 PINCH OF SALT
1 TEASPOON LEMON ZEST
   (GRATED)
2 MEDIUM EGGS
250G PLAIN FLOUR
2 TEASPOON BAKING POWDER
1 SACHET DRIED VANILLA
   CUSTARD POWDER (ENOUGH
   FOR 500ML MILK)
100ML MILK

ICING:
150G ICING SUGAR
3 TEASPOONS LEMON JUICE
FOOD COLOURING

Preheat the oven to 180°C/350°F/Gas Mark 4. Soak the sticks in water to prevent them from burning. Cream together the butter, sugar, salt and lemon zest until light and fluffy. Add the eggs one at a time. Mix the flour with the baking powder and custard powder and add to the mixture. Add the milk until the dough drops heavy from a spoon. With a spoon, place 15 dollops on a baking tray. Stick the skewers into the dough and bake for 15 minutes. Leave to cool on a wire cooling rack. Mix the icing sugar with the lemon juice. Use some of the icing to cover the flat sides of the lollies. Colour the rest of the icing in any colour you like and decorate with dots, lines or whatever you fancy.

Cheeseburger Cakes

Annabel Ferraby

MAKES 12

I got this recipe from a friend I thought they were going to be messy. But they ended up looking like real cheeseburgers!

Make 12 fairy cakes and chocolate brownies using your favourite recipe. Allow to cool to room temperature on a cooling rack. Cut the fairy cakes in half just under the muffin top. Using the bottom layer of the cake and a butter knife, cut the brownies into circles of the same size.
Gently press the brownies at the end to look similar to a burger patty. Colour the coconut with the green food colouring.

To assemble the cheeseburgers: On the bottom 'bun' pipe yellow icing around the outside of the top of the fairy cake and a few zig-zags across the top to help the patty stay in place. Place the brownie 'patty' on top. Pipe red icing for 'ketchup' on top of the patty in the same way. Sprinkle the coconut 'lettuce' on top of the 'patty'. Replace the top of the fairy cake and use a toothpick to hold in place.

12 PLAIN FAIRY CAKES
12 SMALL CHOCOLATE
  BROWNIES
DESICCATED COCONUT
GREEN FOOD COLOURING
RED ICING
YELLOW ICING
12 TOOTHPICKS

Brownies

The Rea Family (Thirza and Eleanor)

MAKES 16-20

We make these brownies shamefully often for ourselves, but they are also great as gifts, and are particularly good rewarmed on a barbecue, which we do every Bonfire Night. The original recipe (from Dan Lepard) includes 125g roughly chopped pecan nuts, but we leave these out for cake-sale purposes and the recipe works just as well without them. Dan Lepard also includes 75ml of bourbon, which definitely would rule them out as a cake-sale offering!

200G DARK CHOCOLATE
125G BUTTER
2 EGGS
125G LIGHT BROWN SOFT
  SUGAR
100G CASTER SUGAR
2 TEASPOONS VANILLA
  ESSENCE
175G PLAIN FLOUR
1 TABLESPOON COCOA

Preheat the oven to 170°C/325°F/Gas Mark 3. Line a 20cm square tin with silver foil. Melt the chocolate with the butter in a saucepan and then remove from the heat. Beat the eggs with both types of sugar until the sugar is dissolved and the mixture is creamy. Beat in the melted butter and chocolate, followed by the vanilla. Sieve the flour and cocoa and add to the chocolate mixture. Spoon the mixture into the tin and bake for 25 minutes, or a little longer if you prefer your brownies more solid.

Lamingtons feature highly in every Australian's childhood! They are little sponge cakes dipped in chocolate icing and then rolled in desiccated coconut (or sprinkles, if they are going to be sold at school). They can also be made with plain sponge cake from the supermarket.

This recipe is from a website about antipodean food (http://australianfoodabout.com).

Lamingtons

The Cruise Family (Katie)

MAKES APPROXIMATELY 20

2 CUPS PLAIN FLOUR
2 TEASPOONS BAKING POWDER
1/4 TEASPOON SEA SALT
2 LARGE EGGS
1/2 CUP BUTTER. SOFTENED
3/4 CUP CASTER SUGAR
1 TEASPOON VANILLA
  EXTRACT
1/2 CUP MILK

2 CUPS OF ICING SUGAR
1/3 CUP OF COCOA POWDER
3 TABLESPOONS BUTTER
1/2 CUP MILK
100-200G DESSICATED
  COCONUT

Preheat the oven to 180°C/350°F/Gas Mark 4. Lightly butter a 20cm (8 inch) square cake tin. In a large bowl, sift together the flour, baking powder and salt. In a separate bowl, use an electric beater to cream the butter and sugar together until pale and fluffy. Then add the eggs one at a time, beating well after each addition. Add the vanilla to the mixture and mix well to combine. Next, use a spatula to alternately add the flour mixture and milk, in three additions, starting and finishing with the flour. Spread the batter into the cake tin, making sure it's evenly spread. Bake in the oven for about 30 minutes. Test the centre of the cake with a toothpick and make sure it comes out clean. Cool the cake in the tin for about 5 minutes and then invert it onto a wire rack to cool. Once the cake has cooled, cut into squares of a desired size and place in an airtight container. Pop the container in the fridge for at least 2 hours or even overnight.

Now for the icing. Place the icing sugar, cocoa powder, butter and milk in a heatproof bowl over a saucepan of simmering water. Stir the mixture until it is smooth but still a bit thick. You don't want the liquid to get too thin otherwise the sponge cake won't absorb the coating. Now it's time to assemble the Lamingtons. Put out some newspaper under wire racks to catch any mess. Place the cake pieces on the racks and have your chocolate icing and desiccated coconut ready. Quickly coat the sponge cake on all sides in the icing mixture and then gently roll the cake in the coconut. Repeat the process. The Lamingtons can be stored in an airtight container for 5 days.

spring
High Days and Holidays

This is a good time of year to reflect on projects and plans for the year ahead — how about starting some new family traditions?
Our experts can help, whether you would like to try making dumplings for Chinese New Year, cooking for your loved one on Valentine's Day or flipping pancakes on Shrove Tuesday!
And why not make bake a cake for someone special on Mother's Day?

Dutch Pancakes

The Vanderkuij Family (Youri)

MAKES APPROXIMATELY 16

Our Dutch pancakes are not like the small, thick ones people in some countries, such as the US, eat for breakfast. Ours are large and thin (a bit like French crepes) and traditionally we have them for tea (never for breakfast!). They are an absolute favourite for children's parties and Sunday nights and in our home they're Daddy's special dish! Traditional toppings are syrup, icing sugar or jam, but you can add savoury fillings if you prefer. We love the combination of apple and fried bacon or pancetta.

```
500G GRAMS PLAIN OR WHOLEMEAL FLOUR
4 LARGE EGGS
1 LITRE MILK
A GOOD PINCH OF SALT
BUTTER OR COOKING OIL FOR FRYING
```

Just mix the ingredients together and you're ready to go. Heat some oil and/or butter in a large frying pan and add a large spoonful of batter. Fry on medium heat until the batter is no longer runny and flip over. The pancakes are done when they are golden brown on both sides. Add a topping and eat while still hot.

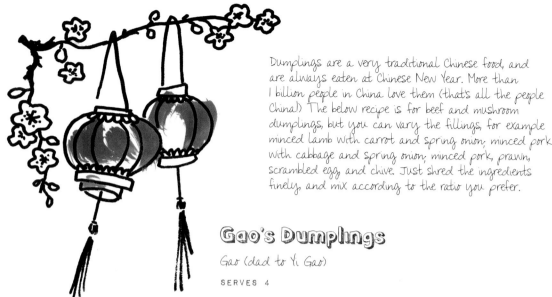

Dumplings are a very traditional Chinese food, and are always eaten at Chinese New Year. More than 1 billion people in China love them (that's all the people China!) The below recipe is for beef and mushroom dumplings, but you can vary the fillings, for example minced lamb with carrot and spring onion; minced pork with cabbage and spring onion; minced pork, prawn, scrambled egg and chive. Just shred the ingredients finely, and mix according to the ratio you prefer.

Gao's Dumplings

Gao (dad to Yi Gao)

SERVES 4

700G PLAIN FLOUR
200G MUSHROOMS, FINELY MINCED
2 ONIONS, FINELY MINCED
400G MINCED BEEF
5 TEASPOONS SALT
1 TEASPOON BLACK PEPPER
5 TEASPOONS OYSTER SAUCE
4 TABLESPOONS VEGETABLE OIL

Put the flour into a large mixing bowl and mix with enough water to form a dough. Place the dough onto a floured work surface and knead for approximately 5 minutes until reasonably smooth and soft, then leave in an oiled bowl covered with a tea towel. To make the filling, mix the beef, mushroom, onion, salt, pepper, oyster sauce and vegetable oil together. Cut the dough in half and roll each half into a long sausage shape. Slice into small pieces, about 3cm thick, and roll each piece into a flat circle shape, about 2mm thick. These are called the 'wrappers'. Put a heaped teaspoon of filling in the middle of each wrapper, then bring the two halves of the wrapper together and press together to seal. Ta-dah! You've made dumplings!

To cook, half fill a deep pot with water and bring to the boil. Once it is boiling, put the dumplings in. Wait until the water reaches boiling point again, then pour a medium-sized glass of cold water into the pot to lower the temperature of the water. Repeat this process two further times. Once the water has come to the boil after the third glass of water has been added, remove dumplings from the pan with a slotted spoon and serve. (NB dumplings should be piping hot inside.) Enjoy with soy sauce.

Step 1:

Step 2:

Step 3:

Step 4:

Step 5:

Step 6:

Step 7:

Step 8:

Step 9:

Step 10:

Step 11:

Step 12: Enjoy!

It's Valentine's Day! How about making a meal for a special person?

mr Ball's
Sea Bass with Butter and Lemon Sauce

Mr Ball (Bishop Gilpin Headteacher)

SERVES 2

This is a recipe I have up my sleeve for when it's my turn to do the cooking. It's quite a good one for Valentine's Day...

2 SEA BASS FILLETS
500G NEW POTATOES
ASPARAGUS TIPS
A COUPLE OF SPRIGS OF
    ROSEMARY. LEAVES REMOVED
    AND ROUGHLY CHOPPED
SALT
LARGE KNOB OF BUTTER
1/2 LEMON. JUICED

Preheat the oven to 200°C/400°F/Gas Mark 6. Par-boil the new potatoes, then drain and place in a roasting tin. Drizzle with olive oil, sprinkle over salt and rosemary and roast for approximately 35 minutes, or until golden brown and crispy. Put butter and lemon juice into a frying pan and heat until butter is melted and starting to sizzle.

Place the sea bass fillets skin down into the pan and cook for approximately 5 minutes. Remove pan from heat, turn the fillets over and allow to sit in the pan for another minute or two, where they will continue to cook.

Boil the asparagus tips in salted water for approximately 5 minutes. Check the sea bass fillets are cooked through prior to serving, then place on plate with potatoes and asparagus, and drizzle with the butter and lemon sauce.

Mousse de Maracuj
(Passion Fruit Mousse)

The Knochenhauer Family

SERVES 4

This is one of the most common ways to serve passion fruit in Brazil. It is extremely easy to prepare and dependably delicious. There are a number of Portuguese shops in London, which sell Brazilian ingredients, but the passion fruit coulis sold in major supermarkets works very well.

1 CUP (250 ML) WHIPPING
    CREAM
1 CUP (250 ML) SWEETENED
    CONDENSED MILK
1/2 CUP (125 ML) FROZEN
    PASSION FRUIT JUICE
    CONCENTRATE OR FRESH
    PASSION FRUIT COULIS
    (AVAILABLE IN
    SOME SUPERMARKETS)
1 WHOLE PASSION FRUIT

Put all the ingredients in a blender, and blend at low speed until the liquid becomes light and fluffy. Pour the mixture into a serving bowl, or individual dessert dishes. If fresh passion fruit is available, spread a small amount of pulp, including seeds on top of the mixture. Chill for at least 2 hours prior to serving.

mr rob's
Steak and Chips

Rob Baughurst (Bishop Gilpin Site Manager)

SERVES 2

This recipe serves two people, or me if I am very hungry.
I like to serve with fresh tomatoes, which I cook on the griddle
with the steak

2 STEAKS (I PREFER
  SIRLOIN, BUT ANY TYPE
  IS FINE)
SOY SAUCE
TERIYAKI SAUCE
WORCESTER SAUCE
VEGETABLE OIL
6 MEDIUM POTATOES
SALT AND PEPPER AND
  MALT VINEGAR TO TASTE

Put a large splash of soy sauce, another of teriyaki and another of Worcester sauce into a large plastic container. Put steak in, turn to coat and leave to marinate in fridge. I put mine in to marinate the night before, but any amount of time is better than none. Peel the potatoes and cut to your preferred chip size. I like mine about 1cm, but thicker or thinner are both ok. It's your meal – have it how you want. Heat vegetable oil in a chip pan until it's very hot (a deep saucepan will do if you don't have a chip pan) and carefully put your chips in. This is the part where I always get splatter burns. (Perhaps an oven glove should be my next purchase!)

Fry hard for just a minute or so then take the chips out and shake off any excess oil. Leave to cool and turn oil down half-way. When chips have cooled considerably, refry until cooked through. This shouldn't take more than a couple more minutes but will vary depending on the thickness of your chips. When you put your chips on for the second time, put a griddle pan on the highest heat and wait until it's smoking hot. Take the steaks from the fridge and turn over again to make sure they are nicely covered in your marinade. Put straight onto the smoking hot griddle for 1-2 minutes and then turn. Cook to your preference (I like mine rare) and plate up with your chips, with salt and pepper to taste, and, of course, vinegar for the chips.

Tuna Sashimi

Cis (mum to Tijmen and Luitzen de Boer)

SERVES 2

This starter is the best tuna you'll ever have!

Rub 2 pieces of good quality fresh tuna steak (not from a supermarket) with a marinade made from 4 tablespoons olive oil, 1 tablespoon sesame oil, 2 tablespoons soy sauce, 1 tablespoon lemon juice, 2 red chillis (seeds removed and cut into small pieces), 4 tablespoons chopped coriander and a thumb-size piece of ginger (cut into small thin pieces). Leave for 2 hours in the fridge (turn the tuna a couple of times, making sure that it is completely coated). Remove from the fridge 10 minutes before serving and serve whole.

BY SOFIA

"if i knew you were comin' i'd've baked a cake"...

Afternoon tea

Mother's Day is a good time to show your gratitude to a special person who takes special care of you. But saying thank you shouldn't be a sentiment reserved for just one day nor for just one person. Making a cake for someone is a very eloquent way of saying "I appreciate you", so we threw a tea-party for our wonderful staff team at Bishop Gilpin, using the following delicious recipes.
Who will you bake a cake for?!

This is a Mary Berry favourite with both our family and Bishop Gilpin mums at coffee mornings! It is really easy to make, as all the ingredients are just put in together and then mixed, and it makes a very light sponge. You can easily adapt it to a lemon sponge (adding grated lemon rind), chocolate sponge (by adding cocoa and boiling water), and either fill it with jam or buttered icing. Best eaten fresh!

All-in-one Victoria Sandwich

The Clapp family (Matthew and Isabel)

MAKES 1 X 20CM (8IN) CAKE

225G (8OZ) BUTTER, SOFTENED
(OR SOFT MARGARINE)
225G (8OZ) CASTER SUGAR
4 EGGS
225G (8OZ) SELF-RAISING FLOUR
3-4 TABLESPOONS RASPBERRY JAM
ICING SUGAR TO DUST

Pre-heat the oven to 180°C/350°F/Gas Mark 4. Grease two 20cm (8in) sandwich tins. Measure the butter, sugar, eggs, flour and baking powder into a large bowl and beat well until thoroughly blended (I use my electric mixer and beat for about 2 minutes). Divide the mixture evenly between the tins and level out. Bake for about 25 minutes or until well risen and the tops of the cakes spring back when lightly pressed with a finger. Leave to cool in the tins for a few moments then turn out, peel off the paper and finish cooling on a wire rack. When completely cold, sandwich the cakes together with the jam. Sprinkle the top with caster or icing sugar and serve and enjoy.

"I WOULD INVITE THE QUEEN FOR TEA. WE WOULD HAVE SANDWICHES, WITH SCONES, JAM AND BUTTER FOR PUDDING (SO TEMPTING!)."

Abigail Bryan-Harris

This recipe is our favourite cake of all time and comes from The DK Children's Baking Book by Denise Smart. We use Delia Smith's chocolate icing recipe. Make the icing first as it takes a while to cool and thicken. (If you make a double batch, it lasts in the fridge for several weeks.) One day Nick plans to make this cake for Paul and Mary on Junior Bake Off...

Nick Long's Chocolate Fudge Cake

The Long family (Nick and Michael)

MAKES 1 X 20CM (8IN) CAKE

CAKE:
175G SOFTENED BUTTER
175G SOFT BROWN SUGAR
150G SELF-RAISING FLOUR
25G COCOA POWDER
1 TABLESPOON BAKING POWDER
   (YES, IT IS A TABLESPOON!)
1/2 TEASPOON BICARBONATE
   OF SODA
3 MEDIUM EGGS
100ML SOUR CREAM

ICING:
75G GRANULATED SUGAR
75ML EVAPORATED MILK
100G PLAIN CHOCOLATE,
   IN SMALL CUBES
40G BUTTER
2 DROPS VANILLA ESSENCE

Preheat the oven to 170°C/325°F/Gas Mark 3 and grease and line the bases of two 20cm (8in) cake tins. Place the butter and sugar in a mixing bowl and whisk together until pale and fluffy. Sift over the flour, cocoa powder, baking powder and bicarbonate of soda.
Add the eggs and sour cream and whisk until combined. Divide the mixture between the two tins and level the tops. Bake for 25-30 minutes then leave to cool for 5-10 minutes in the tins before peeling off the greaseproof paper and turning out onto a wire cooling rack. Ice and decorate when cool.

Combine the sugar and evaporated milk in a heavy saucepan. Place over a low heat and allow sugar to dissolve, stirring frequently. Once dissolved, bring to the boil and simmer gently for 6 minutes without stirring. Take off the heat and put in the chocolate, stirring gently until melted, then stir in the butter and vanilla essence. Transfer the mixture to a bowl, cool, then cover with cling film and chill in the fridge for an hour or so, until it has thickened to a spreadable consistency. (NB If it gets too stiff to spread, you can put it in the microwave for a few seconds to loosen it up.)

Carrot Cake

Sarah (mum to Tilly and Scout Cragg)

MAKES 1 X 20CM (8IN) CAKE

My late mother loved cooking and spent her life in the kitchen creating very traditional food, including suet puddings, savoury pies and a mean quiche. Even now I miss her Sunday lunches, which always had me and my two sisters religiously driving home every week, salivating at the wheel. Her kitchen was the heart of the house and beat with her – a seamless drum of activity which still makes me smile when I think of it. She passed on her love of baking to me and I hope some of that passion rubs off on my two little girls, Tilly and Scout. This recipe, taken from The Hummingbird Bakery Cookbook by Tarek Malouf, is a favourite with our family and really easy to make as you literally throw all the ingredients into a bowl and mix together. It also has the 'wow' factor, as it is stacked three layers deep and completely covered in cream cheese frosting.

CAKE:
300G SOFT LIGHT BROWN SUGAR
3 EGGS
300ML SUNFLOWER OIL
300G PLAIN FLOUR
1 TEASPOON OF BICARBONATE
   OF SODA
1 TEASPOON OF BAKING POWDER
1 TEASPOON GOUND CINNAMON
   PLUS EXTRA TO DECORATE
1/2 TEASPOON GROUND GINGER
1/2 TEASPOON SALT
1/4 TEASPOON OF VANILLA
   EXTRACT
300G CARROTS GRATED
100G SHELLED WALNUTS,
   CHOPPED PLUS EXTRA,
   CHOPPED AND WHOLE
   TO DECORATE

CREAM CHEESE FROSTING:
600G ICING SUGAR
100G UNSALTED BUTTER AT
   ROOM TEMPERATURE
250G CREAM CHEESE (COLD)

Preheat the oven to 170°C/325°F/Gas Mark 3. Line the bases of 3 20cm (8in) cake tins with greaseproof paper. Put the sugar, eggs and oil in a freestanding electric mixer with a paddle attachment (or use a hand-held electric whisk) and beat until all the ingredients are well incorporated (don't worry if the mixture looks slightly split). Slowly add the flour, bicarbonate of soda, baking powder, cinnamon, ginger, salt and vanilla extract and continue to beat until well mixed. Stir in the grated carrots and walnuts by hand until they are all evenly dispersed. Pour the mixture into the prepared cake tins and smooth over with a palette knife. Bake in the preheated oven for 20-25 minutes, or until golden brown and the sponge bounces back when touched. Leave the cakes to cool slightly in the tins before turning out onto a wire cooling rack to cool completely.

For the frosting: Beat the icing sugar, butter and cream cheese together in a freestanding electric mixer with a paddle attachment (or use a hand-held electric whisk) on a medium to slow setting until the mixture comes together and is well mixed. Turn the mixer up to medium-high speed. Continue beating until the frosting is light and fluffy, around 3-5 minutes. Do not over beat as it can quickly become runny.

When the cakes are cold, put one on a cake stand and spread about one quarter of the frosting over it with a palette knife. Place a second cake on top and spread another quarter of the frosting over it. Top with the last cake and spread the remaining frosting over the top and sides. Finish with walnuts and a light sprinkling of cinnamon.

BY JESICA

Fay Ripley's Lemon and Raspberry Cakes

The Reed Family (Poppy, Millie and Nell)

MAKES 8

This recipe is a family favourite and one the girls ask for over and over again. We most often have them warm for pudding with fresh raspberries and cream but they are just as good cold with a cup of tea. Although best made when raspberries are in season, you can use frozen ones too so there is no excuse to not make them all year round! This recipe is from Fay's Family Food by Fay Ripley.

Preheat the oven to 180°C/350°F/Gas Mark 4. Melt the butter and use a little to grease an eight-hole muffin tin. Sift the flour and icing sugar, then add the ground almonds and mix. Whisk the egg whites in another bowl until they form soft peaks. Tip the eggs into the flour mix. Add the lemon zest. Pour in the butter and gently fold with a metal spoon. Pour evenly into the tins and drop 2 raspberries into each cake. Bake for 20 minutes. Cool and turn out. Dust with extra icing sugar when cool.

115G UNSALTED BUTTER
30G PLAIN FLOUR
130G ICING SUGAR
100G GROUND ALMONDS
3 LARGE EGG WHITES
GRATED ZEST OF 2 LEMONS
100G FRESH OR FROZEN
   RASPBERRIES

German Cheesecake

Tina (mum to Zara Roux)

MAKES 1 X 20CM (8IN) CAKE

This is a cake my German mother used to make whenever visitors came over, or for us on Sundays and birthdays. I have kept up the tradition! Sometimes my children will request a different birthday cake, but they always demand this one be served to guests too! This was the first cake we as children learned how to bake as it's so easy, and now Zara often makes it (to great critical acclaim!).

Preheat the oven to 180°C/350°F/Gas Mark 4. Line the base of a 20cm springform tin with greaseproof paper. Mix the ingredients for the base together to form a dough, then press it into the tin with your hand, reserving a few tablespoons to crumble over the top at the end. Bake in the hot oven for 5 minutes. Mix all the filling ingredients together and add to the pre-baked dough, then sprinkle the reserved dough on top. Bake for approximately 40 minutes, until cake no longer wobbles and is golden on top.

BASE:
200G PLAIN FLOUR
100G CASTER SUGAR
1 TEASPOON OF BAKING
   POWDER
125G BUTTER, SOFTENED
1 EGG YOLK
1 TEASPOON VANILLA ESSENCE

FILLING:
1 KG QUARK (AVAILABLE AT
   MOST SUPERMARKETS – DO
   NOT SUBSTITUTE WITH CREAM
   CHEESE OR COTTAGE CHEESE)
4 EGGS PLUS LEFTOVER EGG
WHITE FROM ABOVE
JUICE OF ONE LEMON
200G CASTER SUGAR

Andy is Cornish and this recipe is from his side of the family. They're great to freeze, so I usually make a double batch and then take them out of the freezer when I need them and warm in the oven before serving. We eat them the traditional way, with strawberry jam and lashings of clotted cream. There's an ongoing regional dispute between Devon and Cornwall about whether the jam or the cream goes on first just make sure you do it the proper Cornish way, with jam first then the cream!

Cornish Buttermilk Scones

Simone Tromans (mum to Tom, Alex and Grace)

MAKES APPROXIMATELY 12-15 SMALL SCONES

12 OZ SELF-RAISING FLOUR
1/2 TEASPOON BAKING
   POWDER
PINCH OF SALT
1 1/2 OZ CASTER SUGAR
4 OZ BUTTER
6 OZ BUTTERMILK

Preheat the oven to 220°C/425°F/Gas Mark 7. Lightly grease a baking sheet. Mix the flour, baking powder and salt together and, using fingertips, rub in the butter until the mixture reaches the consistency of breadcrumbs (this can be done in a food processor). Add the buttermilk and gently knead into a soft dough. Roll out on a lightly-floured surface to a thickness of approximately half an inch and cut into rounds using a cutter (I usually use a smallish cutter). Brush the tops with a mixture of beaten egg and milk and bake for 12-15 minutes until golden. Cool on a wire rack, then split in half and serve with jam and cream.

"IF I COULD INVITE ANYONE FOR TEA I WOULD INVITE MAX AND ARTHUR BECAUSE MAX NEEDS TO EAT AND ARTHUR BECAUSE HE IS POLITE."

James Harper-Jones

Baursaks (Mini Doughnuts)

Zeinegul (mum to Ariana)

MAKES A LOT TO SHARE WITH FRIENDS

Baursak in Kazakh means 'aspiration to closeness, unity or feeling part of the family', and no Kazakh party or celebration is complete without them. This little golden doughnut may be one of the most ancient and traditional dishes Kazakhs pass from mothers to daughters, and every family makes them for national holidays or for big occasions. Plain baursaks are usually served with shorpa or meat broth; sweet baursaks with tea and honey or jam, to sweeten the discussions over the table. They can be eaten with any dip or filling: Ariana loves them with melted chocolate! We make them together – she has great fun forming the dough into different shapes.

```
1 CUP (250ML) WARM MILK
1/2 TABLESPOON SALT
1 TABLESPOON SUGAR (OR 3 TABLESPOONS SUGAR
  IF MAKING SWEET BAURSAKS)
1 PACKET DRY YEAST
2 CUPS (500ML) NATURAL DRINKING/POURING YOGHURT
2 EGGS (MEDIUM OR LARGE IS FINE)
50G UNSALTED BUTTER, SOFTENED
3-4 CUPS OF PLAIN FLOUR (APPROXIMATELY 700G)
VEGETABLE OR OLIVE OIL, FOR FRYING
```

Stir the salt, sugar and yeast into the milk and add the yoghurt. In a separate bowl, mix the eggs, butter and flour and slowly stir in the yoghurt mixture, bringing the dough together with your hands to form a ball. You may need to add a little more flour or yoghurt if necessary. Knead for 5 minutes or so until the dough is springy, then wrap in clingfilm and leave in a warm place for 30 or more minutes to rise. When dough has risen, roll into a sausage shape and chop into small bite-sized pieces. Pour oil to a depth of about 3-4cm in a large high-sided pan and heat until a piece of dough sizzles when you drop it into the oil. Cook the barsauks in single-layer batches for approximately 3-4 minutes or until golden. Leave to cool. If making sweet baursaks, dust with icing sugar, drizzle with honey, or inject with jam/cooled melted chocolate.

greek Easter

by Fiona Cunningham

Greece is a unique country. It has over 6,000 islands, of which more than 200 are inhabited, and is a land of stunning natural beauty. Many people are Orthodox Christians and the church plays a massive role in everyone's lives, creating a strong sense of community. The Greeks are intensely patriotic and you see the Greek flag everywhere – even the houses are painted white with blue shutters! They are extremely passionate about everything, especially food.

At no time is this more apparent than at Easter, when passion and community collide in the most extraordinary way. My son Dimitri and I return to Greece every year for Easter, as it's such a special time, and I wanted to capture a little bit of the atmosphere and excitement of the festival for this book.
The only way I was really going to do justice to the food was by cooking it. So we recreated a mini Easter feast for some of the families from the BG Nursery. I think they had a good time!

Why is Easter so special in Greece?

Easter in Greece is a monumental occasion and the whole country celebrates the miracle of Christ (Xristos) coming alive again after His death. The anticipation and sense of occasion is huge and infectious. Everyone becomes very busy to finish whatever they're doing by Easter, and houses are cleaned and prepared for family and guests. The build-up to Christmas in the UK pales in comparison! >>

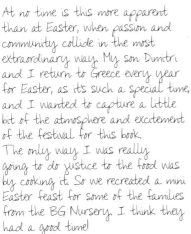

The day before the beginning of Lent, families get together and have a huge feast. From then on until Easter, 40 days later, most Greeks will fast and eat nothing that comes from animals with a blood system: no milk, cheese, yoghurt, eggs, butter, cakes, chocolates, meat or fish. A couple of weeks before Easter, each family will order whole lambs from their local sheep farmer. On the Thursday before Easter Day (Megali Pempti), work stops at midday. Millions of Greeks leave cities for islands or the countryside to celebrate Easter with their families. Whilst the women are busy with food preparations for the big day, children dye eggs bright red to represent the blood of Christ by boiling them with a powdered dye. In the evening, everyone – from babies to octogenarians – gathers late at night at churches in different locations. They follow a large, heavy icon of Christ mounted on a wooden frame and carried by pall-bearers through the streets to mourn Christ's death.

No-one works on Good Friday – it is strictly frowned upon, except for essential services – and ladies of the parish will spend most of the day decorating the icon of Christ with flowers. Later that evening, everybody goes to church to pray and mourn, which is followed by drinking of ouzo or tsiporo (liquor made from the skins and pips of grapes) in the local kafenio (coffee shop).

The next day, Great Saturday (Megalo Sabbato), is a frantically busy day with everyone getting ready for the next day's huge feast. The lamb arrives and is prepared on the spit (a long, heavy steel pole) by the men. The lamb will be cooked over two-metre long metal barrels that have been cut in half lengthways, with the spit resting on grooves in both ends. Wood from olive trees is burned separately to make charcoal, which will be shovelled into the bottom of the barrels the next day to slowly and steadily cook the lamb. During the day, a flame arrives in Greece direct from Jerusalem, and lanterns bearing this flame are sent all around the country by boats or plane. That evening, everyone goes to church and at 11pm there is much happiness as candles are lit from the holy flame, tins of fuel are ignited all along roadsides and up hillsides and mountains and fireworks explode in fantastic displays. After this, restaurants and homes fill up for a meal, which always includes migiritsasoup (cook's soup – made from the stomach and spleen of the lamb) in a dill and avolemono sauce (egg and lemon). Each person takes a red egg from a bowl on the table and taps it end-to-end with each other's egg, to see whose eggs stays un-cracked the longest. Festivities end late at night.

"WHILST THE WOMEN ARE BUSY WITH FOOD PREPARATIONS FOR THE BIG DAY, CHILDREN DYE EGGS BRIGHT RED TO REPRESENT THE BLOOD OF CHRIST BY BOILING THEM WITH A POWDERED DYE."

Easter Day, and everyone is up early. The men light the charcoal and place the spits on the barrel, taking it in turns to continually wind the handle that turns the spit to ensure even cooking of the lamb. (Nowadays some families use machines to do the hard work of turning!) The ladies prepare everything else for the feast on the scale of a military operation. Children run around to each others' houses, and the men may also visit their friends during a break in their cooking duties. The smell of olive wood burning and lamb cooking is tantalising in the extreme. The men and any visitors are supplied with endless wine and meze (snacks) during their time outside cooking the lamb, and much merriment ensues whilst Greek music blares out for all to hear. This often leads to traditional dancing especially when visitors arrive, who also get royally fed and wined. At last, after several hours, the meat is ready. Each spit is taken into the house supported by a man at each end, and carved into thick chunks. Everyone is called to the table and they sit down to a huge feast, which includes lamb, meatballs, pies, soufflé (pasta with ham and cream), chicken, salads, cheeses, sweets, desserts, and litres of wine. Any leftover lamb is eaten cold with salads the next day, or made into a delicious dish called lamb fricassee (lamb cooked with lots of lettuce and fresh dill in an avolemono sauce). Superb!!

Lamb Baked in the Oven (Arni Sto Fourno)

Fiona (mum to Dimitri Cunningham)

SERVES 6 - 8

Preheat the oven to 200°C/400°F/Gas Mark 6. Make deep incisions with a sharp knife all over the flesh and fat of a 2kg leg of lamb and insert slices of fresh garlic – push right in or they'll pop out whilst cooking! Place the lamb in a metal baking dish and rub it with a bit of Greek olive oil, then sprinkle over some sea salt, thyme (dried or several sprigs of fresh) and a touch of paprika. Peel some potatoes, chop in half lengthwise and add to the dish. Pour a large glass of water into the bottom of the pan, along with a dash of red or white wine, and trickle a little olive oil onto the potatoes. Cook in the oven on the middle shelf for about 2 hours, depending on the size and weight of your lamb (adjust cooking times for smaller amounts). If the top of the lamb is looking too browned, cover loosely with foil. Once cooked, leave to rest for 10 minutes. Squeeze half a lemon over the lamb and potatoes whilst still hot, roughly cut into portions and serve, spooning over the liquid in the bottom of the pan. Eat with a Greek salad and tsatsiki.

This is a totally authentic Greek recipe learnt from my husband's 80-year-old Greek aunt who is one of the best cooks I have ever encountered anywhere in the world. A great healthy snack for starving kids, vegetarians or those with low iron levels! It only takes about 10-15 minutes to prepare, and once it's in the oven you can sit back with a nice glass of Ouzo and put your feet up!

Authentic Greek Spanakopita (Spinach and Feta Pie)

Fiona (mum to Dimitri Cunningham)

MAKES 20-25 SMALL SQUARES

1/2 WINE GLASS OLIVE OIL
(PREFERABLY GREEK)
2 SHEETS READY-ROLLED
FRESH SHORT-CRUST OR
PUFF PASTRY (OR MAKE
YOUR OWN IF YOU HAVE
TIME, BUT USING OLIVE
OIL INSTEAD OF BUTTER)
1 LARGE BAG FRESH READY-
WASHED SPINACH LEAVES
(APPROX. 450G)
2 EGGS
200G FETA CHEESE
1/2 BUNCH FRESH SPRING
ONIONS, FINELY SLICED
1 TABLESPOON CHOPPED DILL
(FRESH IS BEST)
SALT AND BLACK PEPPER
TO TASTE

Preheat the oven to 180°C/350°F/ Gas Mark 4. Remove pastry from fridge. Dip a pastry brush in the oil and brush it all over the bottom and sides of a stainless steel baking dish (not glass), of similar size to the sheet of pastry (32cm x 22cm x 5cm). In a very large mixing bowl, throw in the spinach (roughly tear if leaves are large). Open the packet of feta and roughly crumble into the bowl, then add the eggs, spring onions, dill, olive oil (retain the wine glass for later – don't wash it out!) and a couple of pinches of salt and pepper. Line the bottom of the oven dish with a sheet of pastry (it doesn't need to come up the sides because it's not a closed pie). Mix all the ingredients together thoroughly with your hands, then scoop into the dish. Even it out but don't pat down, and don't worry if it only looks half-full, it's meant to be a shallow pie. Cover the pie with the top sheet of pastry, and score (don't cut) with a sharp knife into small portions (this is easier if you start in the middle, making the shape of a cross). Each portion should be about 5cm2.

Add a little milk into the wine glass and mix with any remaining olive oil, then brush across the top of the pastry, taking care not to 'smudge' the scoring. Bake in the oven for approximately 1.5 hours until golden brown, covering with foil if the top starts to get too dark. Remove from oven and allow to cool for 5 minutes, then cut along the score marks and serve warm – utterly delicious! Can be kept at room temperature for a couple of days (if it hasn't already been eaten!) If refrigerated warm for 30 seconds in a microwave before serving. Kali Oreksei!

Real Greek Salad

Fiona (mum to Dimitri Cunningham)

SERVES 6 PEOPLE AS A SIDE SALAD

This is what they make in Greek homes and tavernas in real Greece! It's so easy to make, and the rougher you chop the ingredients, the better it tastes!

6 FRESH VINE OR PLUM
   TOMATOES OR 3 BEEFSTEAK
   TOMATOES (SLIGHTLY SOFT
   AND FULLY RIPE ARE
   THE BEST)
1/2 MEDIUM RED ONION,
   CUT INTO CHUNKY SLICES
200G FETA CHEESE
1 WHOLE CUCUMBER
1/2 GLASS OLIVE OIL
   (PREFERABLY GREEK)
PINCH OF ROUGH SEA SALT
1 TEASPOON OREGANO
1/4 GREEN PEPPER, DICED
   (APPROXIMATELY 1CM2)
A DOZEN OR SO GREEN AND/OR
   BLACK KALAMATA OLIVES
   (HOWEVER YOU LIKE THEM,
   BUT STONES-IN ARE BEST)

Take a medium-sized salad bowl. Chop the tomatoes in half, and remove the green stem. Keeping the half tomato in the palm of your left hand (assuming you're right-handed), cut roughly into 6 or 7 bite-size segments over the bowl, turning the tomato around and around as you cut it. Cut all the half tomatoes this way (not on a board!), adding to the bowl as you go, so that all the juice is collected.
Slice the cucumber in half down its length, then cut across the width in reasonably chunky slices about half a centimetre wide and add to the bowl. Peel the onion, cut in half from top to bottom and slice fairly thickly from top to bottom (the Greeks would also do this in the palm of their hand!) Add to the bowl along with the salt, green pepper and olives, then give everything a short stir and leave for 10-20 minutes to let the salt work into the vegetables. Finally, roughly crumble the feta into large pieces on top of the salad, pour over the olive oil and sprinkle the oregano on top of the feta. Delicious on its own with some crusty bread, or with any dish, particularly lasagne or pasta. Kali Oreksei!

Authentic Greek Tsatsiki

Fiona (mum to Dimitri Cunningham)

SERVES 6 PEOPLE AS AN ACCOMPANIMENT

Tsatsiki can be served with anything at all, from fish fingers to beef steaks. It's good for the health (not so for the breath but who cares!), and is delicious when made properly. In Greece it's put on the plate along with other food, as you would with ketchup, potatoes, vegetables etc., not used solely as a dip (a British thing). Dimitri's favourite combo is fried calamari rings, home-made chips and lashings of tsatsiki. Mine is a good beef steak, home-made chips and tsatsiki. It keeps for quite a few days in the fridge.

500G TOTAL GREEK YOGHURT
   (DON'T USE 'GREEK-STYLE',
   IT DOESN'T WORK!)
6 SMALL OR 3 LARGE CLOVES
   OF GARLIC
1/2 LARGE CUCUMBER
GENEROUS PINCH OF SEA SALT
SPLASH OF VINEGAR
1 TEASPOON OF CHOPPED DILL
   (FRESH IS BEST)
SPLASH OF OLIVE OIL
   (GREEK IS BEST)
1 OLIVE

Grate the cucumber and put into a large sieve over a deep bowl. Let it drain whilst you're preparing the rest of the ingredients, pushing it from time to time with the back of a spoon to get most of the juice out (or the tsatsiki will be too watery). Grate or finely chop the garlic and add to another bowl with the yoghurt, dill, salt, vinegar and cucumber (drink the cucumber juice – it's good for hair and nails!). Mix together, adding more salt or drops of vinegar until you reach the taste you like. Put into a clean bowl, cover with clingfilm and leave in the fridge for flavours to develop. After 20-30 minutes, top with a large splash of olive oil and an olive. Delicious with steaks, sausages, pork or lamb chops, fried calamari, home-made chips or just on its own with some crusty bread. Kali Oreksei!

Easter Biscuits

Basia Pacześna-Vercueil (mum to Sofia, Ania, Derik and Olivia)

Easter in Poland is a vibrant holiday with many traditions and customs. It starts on the Saturday before Easter with Swieconka (Shi-vien-zon-ka), one of the most enduring and beloved Polish traditions, where people take to church baskets of traditional food to be blessed, along with colourful, decorated eggs.

Easter Sunday is spent with our extended families. We share boiled eggs – a piece of egg with salt and pepper, consecrated by a priest in a basket, is an inseparable accessory to the good wishes we extend to each other at Easter – and a huge feast. And, of course, the Easter Bunny also pays a visit! Easter Monday – Lany poniedzialek (lani po-nie-ja-weck) – is celebrated with great enthusiasm by everyone, especially the children, by sprinkling each other with water. Some people say that being splashed with water on this day will bring you good luck throughout the year.

Cakes and cookies play a hugely important role over Easter, and bakeries all over Poland are filled with specially prepared treats. As a child I felt hugely blessed as my grandparents ran a cake shop in a small town called Milanowek, on the outskirts of Warsaw. They met just after the Second World War when they worked in the same bakery and fell in love. With Grandpa Jozio being a master baker they decided to open their own little bakery, which specialised in cakes only. As a little girl I used to love watching my grandparents work and found the bakery the most magical place ever (you can just imagine why)!

I guess love for baking runs in the family and this year the family bakery will be celebrating its 60th birthday! My kids have been helping me with baking and decorating cookies ever since they could climb on a chair and reach the kitchen worktop. I can proudly say that they are the 4th generation of bakers in training!

FOR THE COOKIE DOUGH:
250G UNSALTED BUTTER, SOFTENED
250G PLAIN FLOUR
125G SELF-RAISING FLOUR
120G CASTER SUGAR
1 FREE RANGE EGG YOLK
1 TABLESPOON VANILLA EXTRACT
A PINCH OF SALT

WESOŁEGO ALLELUJA
(VE-SO-WE-GOA ALLE-LU-YAH)
(HAPPY EASTER)

FOR THE ROYAL ICING:
1 LARGE FREE RANGE EGG WHITE
APPROX. 200G ICING SUGAR,
   SIEVED
1 TEASPOON LEMON JUICE
FOOD COLOURING OF YOUR CHOICE

TO DECORATE:
250G COLOURED SUGAR PASTE
   (I USE THE PALE RENSHAW
   RANGE OR WHITE PLUS FOOD
   COLOURING)
COOKIE CUTTERS, A DISPOSABLE
PIPING BAG WITH A FINE NOZZLE
(I USE WILTON 1.5 OR 2) AND
A SMALL FLOWER PLUNGER CUTTER

Cream butter, sugar and vanilla together until light and fluffy. Add egg yolk. Sift the flour and salt and add to the mixture. Stir gently until everything is incorporated, taking care not to overwork the dough. Split the dough into two balls, wrap each tightly in cling film and leave in the fridge to rest for 30 minutes. Preheat the oven to 180°C/350°F/Gas Mark 4. Line three baking sheets with grease-proof paper. Roll out the dough between two sheets of parchment paper (this stops it getting stuck to the rolling pin!) and cut out shapes with the cookie cutters. Bake for about 15 minutes until golden. Cool on a wire rack, whilst trying to prevent your kids from helping themselves to the cookies which have filled the house with their amazing aroma!

To make the royal icing, slowly beat the egg white and lemon juice into the icing sugar until light and fluffy and soft peaks start forming. If you feel the mixture is too watery, just add a bit more icing sugar. NB for a smooth mixture that will not clog the nozzle make sure there are no lumps in the egg white and the bowl is grease free. To decorate, roll out the sugar paste on a lightly floured surface to a thickness of about 3mm. Brush the cookies very lightly with royal icing. Using the same cutter used to create biscuits cut out shapes in the paste and secure in place on the top of the biscuits.

To finish, add a nozzle to the piping bag and fill it half full with royal icing. Do not overfill as it will be difficult to apply a steady pressure to create your designs. For the bunnies I create a little collar, a nose and a tail with royal icing. With a flower plunger cut out few small flowers and decorate as your heart desires.

the Summer term

Head out to Wimbledon Common at the start of the Summer Term and, if you listen carefully, you may hear the song of the cuckoo. The sound heralds the coming of summer, and with it an easier way of life. No-one wants to be slaving over a hot stove when there are outdoor adventures to be had – strawberries to be picked, marshmallows to be toasted and tents to be built in the garden – so we have some ideas for meals which can be rustled up quickly. But, before any of the fun can start, there are a few dreaded exams to get through. We give you some child-friendly recipes for dishes packed full with omega-3 fatty acids (we can't promise that our recipes will make you brainier, but they'll certainly taste good!). Then, when it's time to put the books away, we have some great ideas for al fresco eating: lunchbox tips from our Japanese families, barbecue ideas from our South Africans and party food from around the globe. And not forgetting some healthy (and not so healthy) snack ideas to keep you fuelled for a summer of sport!

Summer time and the living is easy... Here are some dishes that only take minutes to prepare, or which can be started the night before and finished off the next day with the minimum of fuss.

Quick and Easy meals

Cheat's Chicken Korma

Samantha (mum to Millie and Tabitha Wyatt)

SERVES 4-6

This Jamie Oliver recipe is a good one for children as it's not too hot. Although you can add extra chilli. Chicken thighs taste better, in my opinion, but Millie prefers the taste of breast meat. This recipe is also good with prawns. My kids love it, although Tabitha leaves the chickpeas! My stepsons (19 and 22) love it and eat massive plates of it. Tabitha likes to put it all onto a poppadom.

800G SKINLESS AND BONELESS CHICKEN THIGHS OR BREASTS, PREFERABLY FREE-RANGE OR ORGANIC
2 MEDIUM ONIONS
1 SMALL FRESH GREEN CHILLI (OPTIONAL)
THUMB-SIZED PIECE OF FRESH GINGER
SMALL BUNCH OF CORIANDER
400G TIN OF CHICKPEAS
VEGETABLE OIL
KNOB OF BUTTER
1/2 JAR OF PATAK'S KORMA CURRY PASTE
400ML TIN OF COCONUT MILK
SMALL HANDFUL OF FLAKED ALMONDS
2 HEAPED TABLESPOONS DESICCATED COCONUT
SEA SALT AND FRESHLY GROUND BLACK PEPPER

Cut the chicken into 3cm pieces. Peel, halve and finely slice the onions. Halve, de-seed and finely slice the chilli, if you are using it. Peel and finely chop the ginger. Pick the coriander leaves off and finely chop the stalks. Drain the chickpeas. Put a large saucepan on a high heat and add a couple of lugs of oil. Put the chicken thighs into the pan, if using, and brown lightly for 5 minutes (breasts added later). Push the chicken to one side of the pan. Add the onions, ginger, coriander stalks, butter and chilli (if using) and cook for approximately 10 minutes. Keep stirring so the onion doesn't catch but turns golden. Add the korma paste, flaked almonds, chickpeas, coconut milk, coconut and chicken breasts (if using). Half fill the empty chickpea tin with water and stir into the mix. Bring to the boil, then turn the heat down and simmer for half an hour. Check the curry to make sure it's not drying out, adding extra water if necessary. When the chicken is tender and cooked, season carefully with salt and pepper. Serve with rice, poppadoms and mango chutney. Yum!

Minimal Washing-up Chicken Dinner

Louise Cooper (mum to Cerys and Dylan Cooper Jones)

SERVES 4

The original recipe came from a book-club dinner, but I adapt it to include whatever is in my fridge. And as a working mother, the big advantage is that it only requires one pan to wash up. The original contains chorizo but my husband doesn't eat red meat so we eat it without. However you can add tomatoes, courgettes, carrots or basically whatever is in your fridge drawer. Both my children love the recipe, although we have to hide the aubergine under the chicken to get Dylan to eat it!

OUR MUM COOKS THIS TOO BUT SHE ADDS TWO TABLESPOONS OF BALSAMIC VINEGAR AND HALF A TEASPOON OF SMOKED PAPRIKA TO HER VERSION. WE THINK IT'S YUMMY!
The Doerflers

4-8 CHICKEN THIGHS OR DRUMSTICKS (OR AS MANY AS YOUR FAMILY REQUIRES)
3 OR 4 ONIONS, QUARTERED
5 GARLIC CLOVES, WHOLE
2 OR 3 RED PEPPERS, CUT INTO LARGE SLICES
1 AUBERGINE, CUT INTO FAT SLICES
8-10 SMALL POTATOES CUT IN HALF
OLIVE OIL
SALT, PEPPER AND ROBUST HERBS SUCH AS THYME OR ROSEMARY TO TASTE

Preheat the oven to 180°C/350°F/Gas Mark 4. Put all the ingredients in a roasting tin, with many generous slugs of olive oil, salt and plenty of black pepper and any herbs you fancy. Cook for approximately 40 minutes to 1 hour or until the chicken is thoroughly cooked through and golden.

This is a recipe that is easy to prepare for a weekend supper with friends but one that the children will also enjoy! It can be prepared the night before and heated up on the day (ensure chicken is piping hot).

Creamy Mustard and Tarragon Chicken

The Haynes family (Harry and Freddie)

SERVES 4

```
3 TABLESPOONS VEGETABLE OIL
1 ONION, CHOPPED
1 GARLIC CLOVE, CRUSHED
2 MEDIUM LEEKS, SLICED
4 MEDIUM CARROTS, ROUGHLY DICED
4 BONELESS CHICKEN THIGHS, SKIN REMOVED
4 CHICKEN DRUMSTICKS, SKIN REMOVED
1 1/2 LEVEL TABLESPOONS PLAIN FLOUR
300ML (1/2  PINT) CIDER
300ML (1/2  PINT) CHICKEN STOCK
3 LEVEL TABLESPOONS DIJON MUSTARD
200ML CRÈME FRAICHE
4 LEVEL TABLESPOONS CHOPPED FRESH TARRAGON
```

Heat 1 tablespoon of oil in a large flameproof casserole dish or pan. Add the onion and cook over a medium heat for 4-5 minutes. Add the garlic and cook for 1 minute. Add the carrots and cook for five minutes. Then add the leeks and continue to cook, covered, for 5 minutes so the vegetables soften slightly.

Meanwhile, add the remaining oil to a large non-stick frying pan and brown the chicken all over in batches. Set aside. Stir flour into the pan containing the vegetables and cook for 1 minute. Stir in the cider, chicken stock and mustard and season well with salt and freshly ground pepper. Add the chicken pieces, then cover and bring to the boil. Reduce the heat and simmer for 20-25 minutes or until the chicken is tender. Stir in the crème fraiche and tarragon and heat through for a couple of minutes.

This tart – a version of one I came across on a French cooking course I did with my mother a few years ago – has been cooked and enjoyed many times with family and friends, especially in the summer months. Delicious with a green salad, such as rocket and Parmesan, it makes a great vegetarian option. Can be eaten hot or cold.

Quick Tomato Tart

Zoe Bulman (mum to Charles and Millie)

SERVES 6

350G PUFF PASTRY
1.5KG TOMATOES, SLICED TO A THICKNESS OF APPROXIMATELY 1/2CM
150G MASCARPONE
50G FRESH PARMESAN, FINELY GRATED
1 LARGE BUNCH FRESH BASIL, LEAVES PICKED FROM THE STALK AND FINELY SLICED
SALT AND FRESHLY GROUND PEPPER

Preheat the oven to 200°C/400°F/Gas Mark 6. Line a baking tray with baking parchment. On a lightly-floured surface, roll the pastry into a rectangle about half a centimetre thick (or a circle slightly larger than 30cm if you want it to look really pretty). Put it on the baking tray, cover with cling film and let it rest in the fridge for 20 minutes. Mix mascarpone, Parmesan and basil together and season well. Remove the pastry from the fridge and spread with the mascarpone mix, leaving a 10cm gap around the edges. Crimp the edges with your thumb and forefinger. Layer the sliced tomatoes over the top neatly. Return it to the tray and bake in the preheated oven for 30 minutes, then turn the temperature down to 150°C and cook for a further 45 minutes. The tart is done when the base is crisp and there is no liquid left in the tomatoes.

My brother, Matt, introduced me to the idea of making my own pizza dough. He even gave me my own electric pizza oven, but you can get great results using your normal oven – it's the homemade dough that makes the difference. It only takes 30 minutes or so to prove the dough – you can make the tomato sauce topping during this time (or just use passata straight from the jar if you are in a real rush).

My children like to chop all their favourite toppings – most of them are easy to slice so they can get through them without using a sharp knife – and put them in separate bowls so they can pick out their choices easily. Just don't load up the pizza base with too many toppings or it will make the base soggy! You can make the dough and the sauce the night before and refrigerate overnight, which means you only have a very quick assembly job the next day. The dough and sauce also freeze well.

Preston-style Pizza

Katie (mum to Gabriel and Nellie Weston)

MAKES 4 INDIVIDUAL PIZZAS

PIZZA DOUGH:
500G STRONG WHITE BREAD
   FLOUR (OR 400G FLOUR
   AND 100G FINE SEMOLINA,
   WHICH MAKES THE DOUGH
   A BIT MORE ROBUST)
1/2 TABLESPOON SALT
1 SACHET (7G) INSTANT
   YEAST
1/2 TABLESPOON CASTER
   SUGAR
325ML WATER
A GLUG OF OLIVE OIL

TASTY TOMATO SAUCE:
2 SHALLOTS
1 CLOVE GARLIC
2 SLICES BACON OR
   PANCETTA (OPTIONAL)
400G PASSATA OR TINNED
   TOMATOES
1 TEASPOON SUGAR
SALT AND PEPPER TO TASTE
3 OR 4 FRESH BASIL LEAVES

PIZZA TOPPINGS ACCORDING
TO PREFERENCE, EG MUSH-
ROOMS, HAM, SALAMI,
SPRING ONIONS, SLICED
PEPPERS, OLIVES, TINNED
TUNA, GRATED MOZZARELLA
CHEESE

Measure out the flour and salt in a big bowl. In a jug measure out 325ml warm water (or weigh it as 325g) and mix in the yeast and sugar. Pour the liquid into the dry ingredients and mix together.

Once it's all combined, stir in the olive oil. Turn out the dough onto a floured surface and knead it for about 10 minutes. Hold onto one side of the dough ball and push the other away with the heel of your hand, keeping your fingers relaxed and open. You can tell the dough's ready when the texture turns from lumpy and porridgy to silky smooth. Flour the big bowl and put the dough back in and cover with a damp tea towel. Leave to prove in a warm, draught-free place (like inside the microwave) for 30 minutes or so, until doubled in size and dough doesn't spring back when you make a hole in it with your finger.

While the dough's proving you can make the tomato topping for your pizza. Finely chop the shallots and garlic and gently fry, with bacon, for five minutes until the onion is soft. Add the passata, sugar, salt and pepper and cook for five minutes, then tear up and add the basil leaves.

Preheat the oven to 250°C/500°F/Gas Mark 9 or the highest heat possible. Turn dough onto a floured surface and divide into four equal parts. Squash each ball flat to get rid of the air and then roll it back into a tight ball.

Leave for another 10 minutes while you dust 4 pizza tins or 2 large baking sheets with flour and/or semolina. Dust your worktop with flour and/or semolina and take a piece of dough. Squash it flat with your fingers, then roll out with a floured rolling pin until it's about half a centimetre thick. Place on baking sheets. Add a tablespoon or so of tomato topping and spread it around. Then add your chosen toppings, finishing off with a scattering of mozzarella cheese (called pizza cheese in our house). Put the pizza in the oven for about 10 minutes, or until the cheese is bubbling and going brown.

"IF I COULD HAVE ANY MEAL ON MY BIRTHDAY
I WOULD PROBABLY GO FOR PIZZA"

Mia Bevan

I was born in one of the most beautiful places in the whole world – Kisoro, in Western Uganda, on the border with Congo and Rwanda. It was a privilege to grow up in such an idyllic setting, under the peaks of the beautiful Mufumbiro Mountains, home to the famous and now protected Mountain Gorillas. But life wasn't easy in Uganda under Idi Amin, and, after completing my studies in Kampala I, along with thousands of others, fled the country to escape persecution. After managing to survive 21 check points on the way out of the country, I finally arrived on safer shores here in Britain. I knew I wanted to work with food; I taught myself to cook from an early age and have always loved cooking. I spent 15 years working as a butcher, then I worked my way up through the ranks of a catering company, from where it was a happy hop, skip and jump over to Bishop Gilpin.

I have many fond memories of my 10 years at the school, including being asked for this dish all the time! I decided to choose this recipe as it was a perennial favourite with the children and as popular in the middle of winter as on a hot sunny day.

Ben's
Tuna Pasta

Noshadali Kadan, otherwise known as Ben, our much loved school cook, who retired for health reasons in 2013.

SERVES 4-5

500G PASTA
3 X 160G CANS DOLPHIN-
  FRIENDLY TUNA IN SPRING
  WATER OR BRINE, DRAINED
500G FROZEN SWEETCORN
1 SMALL JAR MAYONNAISE
  (OR ENOUGH TO GET
  A CREAMY CONSISTENCY)

Boil the pasta according to the packet instructions and drain. Steam the sweetcorn until cooked and drain. Break up the tuna into small flakes. Combine the pasta, tuna and sweetcorn and mix with sufficient mayonnaise to achieve the desired consistency. Season to taste.

Here are some other easy pasta ideas...

Pasta Iris

Liam (dad to Iris Russell)

This very easy quick and tasty dish is named after my daughter and is really just some of her favourite flavours on pasta. Cook your pasta add some olive oil, mill some black pepper, squeeze half a lemon and a handful of Parmesan cheese. Mix together and serve. Obviously add as much of each flavour according to personal taste.

Pasta Zetidi

The Clapp family (Matthew and Isabel)

SERVES 5

Some years ago we stayed in southern Corsica. This meal came about as a result of the ingredients that happened to be available both on our arrival in Villa Zetidi and from a small local supermarket. We all enjoyed the result on our first evening! It's a great meal for using up whatever happens to be in the fridge or cupboard at the time and is a family favourite. Best eaten outside (if possible on a sunny Mediterranean terrace)!

375G SPAGHETTI
1 ONION
2 RED PEPPERS
2 LARGE CARROTS, DICED
5 SLICES OF HAM
1 JAR TOMATO SAUCE,
  EG PROVENCAL
EXTRA TOMATO PUREE AS NEEDED
1 TEASPOON MIXED HERBS
FRESH PARMESAN TO SERVE

Boil the spaghetti as per the packet instructions. In a separate pan, fry the onion to soften, add the carrots and cook for 3 minutes or so to soften slightly. Then add all other ingredients and cook for 10 minutes. Pour over the sauce and serve with Parmesan cheese.

Easy Lime Cheesecake

The Wheatley family (Isabella)

SERVES 8

This is our favourite cheesecake recipe, adapted from a Waitrose recipe card. It's easy to make and never fails to delight. We vary the recipe using different flavoured jellies. Kids love making it too.

50G UNSALTED BUTTER,
  CUT INTO CHUNKS
150G PACK CHOCOLATE CHIP
  COOKIES, CRUSHED
135G PACK LIME JELLY,
  CUT INTO SMALL PIECES
1/2 X 410G CAN EVAPORATED
  MILK, CHILLED
200G PACK SOFT CHEESE
3 LIMES

Line the base of a 20cm x 5cm round loose-bottomed sandwich tin with baking parchment. Melt the butter in a saucepan and stir in the crushed biscuits. Press the mixture into the base of the prepared sandwich tin and chill. In a bowl, dissolve the jelly in 100ml boiling water. Stir and then set aside to cool.

Meanwhile, whisk the evaporated milk in a large bowl using an electric or balloon whisk, until light and fluffy, and doubled in volume. Then whisk in the cream cheese until smooth and well combined. Take the finely grated zest and juice of 2 of the limes. Finely slice the remaining lime and set aside. Add all the juice and half of the zest to the cream cheese mix then whisk in the jelly. (Keep the rest of the zest chilled.) Pour over the biscuit base and chill for 2 hours or until set. Decorate with the reserved lime zest and slices of lime.

White Chocolate and Raspberry Brioche Pudding

Siobhan (mum to Imogen Holmes)

SERVES 4-6

This recipe from my sister-in-law is the easiest pudding I've ever made and tastes fabulous. Definitely one that the kids can make. We usually serve it to friends and family when they come for lunch or supper, and everyone loves it! It's very healthy as there are lots of raspberries and all that calcium from the chocolate and double cream!

2 PUNNETS RASPBERRIES
8 BRIOCHE ROLLS, SLICED
200G WHITE CHOCOLATE
600ML DOUBLE CREAM

Preheat the oven to 180°C/350°F/Gas Mark 4. Cover the base of an ovenproof dish (I use my medium-sized lasagne dish) with raspberries. Place slices of brioche on top. Melt the chocolate with the cream in a heatproof bowl set over a saucepan of gently simmering water, stirring until smooth. Pour over the brioche, ensuring each slice is coated. Cook for 15-30 minutes until golden.

Edd's Toblerone Pudding

Elizabeth Broad. (Taken from the first Bishop Gilpin cookbook, edited by Barbara Zarzycki and Rose Williams, July 2002).

SERVES 6

200G TOBLERONE
10FL OZ WHIPPING CREAM
CHOCOLATE FLAKE, TO
  DECORATE (OPTIONAL)

Gently melt the Toblerone in a heatproof bowl over a pan of simmering water. Whip the cream and add to the melted chocolate, a little at a time. Distribute mix equally in 6 ramekins and refrigerate until required. Decorate with crumbled chocolate flake, and serve with cream.

Swedish Gino (White Chocolate Fruit Gratin)

The Josefsson family (Gustav)

This Swedish classic – named after the Italian chef who made it popular – is the yummiest and fastest dessert you will ever make! We like to make this as it's easy, the whole family can help with its preparation and everybody loves the end result! It's nice to use fruit in season, eg strawberries in summer or apples and pears in autumn, but any fruit works. For a more grown-up taste try with fresh figs, or mix flavourings such as grated ginger, desiccated coconut or fresh mint into the fruit, or flaked almonds in with the chocolate. Also works well on the barbecue (bake in the indirect heat of a covered barbecue, to the side of the coals; we use un-lidded disposable foil containers).

FRESH FRUIT, EG STRAWBERRIES, BANANAS, KIWIS
JUICE OF 1 LIME (OR LEMON)
100-200G WHITE CHOCOLATE, GRATED (EASIER IF YOU FREEZE FOR 30 MINUTES BEFORE GRATING!)

Preheat the oven to 200°C/400°F/Gas Mark 6. Peel the fruit and cut into bite-sized pieces – children love to help with this! Put the fruit into an ovenproof dish, squeeze over the lime juice and distribute the chocolate evenly over the top. Bake in the oven for around 10 minutes until the chocolate starts to turn golden, but watch closely to avoid burning! Serve straight from the oven with vanilla ice cream, yogurt or custard.

Finnish Blueberry Dessert

Christelle (mum to Jasper and Sofia Heikkila)

SERVES 4

This is a really simple but delicious recipe from Finland. It contains an ingredient that all Finns are obsessed with – blueberries (when a blueberry pie flavoured ice cream was introduced in Finland it became their best selling flavour of all time!). Whilst this is perfect for summer when wild Finnish blueberries are in abundance, my mother-in-law often makes this with frozen blueberries at Christmas time (no Christmas pudding for the Finns). Of course, this dessert can be made with any berries, and if you are worried about your waistline you can use a lower-fat cream substitute. You could also experiment with some vanilla sugar and some creative toppings.

250G QUARK
200ML WHIPPING CREAM
2 TABLESPOONS OF SUGAR
300ML BLUEBERRIES

Whisk the cream in a large bowl until thick, but not too stiff. Then whisk in the quark, sugar and blueberries. Leave in the fridge for a few minutes before serving in individual bowls. Decorate with blueberries.

The days are long, the sky is blue and the temperature is hot, hot, hot! It can only mean one thing: exam time! Emerging evidence shows that omega-3 fatty acids – found in fish, for example – may have a role to play in the development of the immune system and cognitive functions. Here are some child-friendly fish recipes with which to nourish your hard-workers.

BISHOP GILPIN

Brain food

Fried Prawns with Wasabi Mayonnaise

Maria (mum to Jessica Susanto)

SERVES 2-3

I love food: eating it, writing about it and photographing it! This is the sort of thing I typically cook at home: easy cooking with an Asian feel (reflecting our Indonesian background), but using a mix of eastern and western ingredients. I don't usually measure ingredients, but I have tried to give quantities for the purposes of the book.

400G RAW KING PRAWNS
200G PLAIN FLOUR
PINCH OF SALT, GROUND
  PEPPER AND SUGAR
  (FOR PRAWNS AND MAYO)
3-4 TABLESPOONS MAYONNAISE
JUICE OF 1 LEMON
WASABI PASTE, TO YOUR
  TASTE (IT DEPENDS
  HOW ADVENTUROUS
  YOUR CHILDREN ARE!)
VEGETABLE OIL, FOR FRYING

Put the mayonnaise, lemon juice and wasabi paste in a bowl and stir together well. Add a pinch of sugar and salt (to taste). Put the flour, salt, sugar and pepper in a bowl, give a good mix and add the prawns, stirring well to coat. Add enough oil to cover the prawns in a pan and heat until a small piece of bread sizzles when dropped in. (NB Hot oil can be dangerous – do not leave unattended.) Carefully lower prawns into the hot oil and fry for 2-3 minutes, until the inside is piping hot and the outside is crisp and golden. Remove with a slotted spoon and place on a paper towel to absorb excess oil. Serve with rice and the wasabi mayonnaise.

Easy Fish Pie

The Tindale-Paul family (Luke and Josh)

SERVES 4

This is so delicious that both adults and children alike will usually want seconds. Originally found in a magazine, it has been a family favourite in the Tindale-Paul household for several years now. It is easy to make and very versatile: it can be made as individual fish pies for children's tea, enjoyed as a family meal or dressed up for guests.

3 LARGE FLOURY POTATOES,
  PEELED AND CUBED
100G BROCCOLI
OLIVE OIL
HANDFUL OF WASHED,
  SHREDDED LEEKS
1 GARLIC CLOVE, FINELY CHOPPED
400G MIXED FISH (WHITE, SALMON,
  SMOKED HERRING – WHATEVER
  YOU FANCY. I OFTEN USE THE
  FROZEN FISH PIE MIX FROM
  A LOCAL SUPERMARKET)
100G SMALL COOKED PRAWNS
HANDFUL OF SPINACH, WASHED
  AND CHOPPED
3 TABLESPOONS CRÈME FRAICHE
1 1/2 TEASPOONS MUSTARD POWDER
SALT AND PEPPER

Preheat the oven to 180°C/350°F/Gas Mark 4. Start to cook the potato cubes in a pan of boiling water. After around 8 minutes add the broccoli and cook for 4 minutes, taking care not to overcook it. Drain and mash with a small splash of olive oil. Set aside. In a large pan heat the olive oil and add the leeks and garlic. When they have softened, add the fish, prawns and spinach and cook on a medium heat for 3-4 minutes. Reduce the heat and add the crème fraiche, mustard powder and seasoning. Stir through, then remove from the heat and either pour into one large pie dish or divide between four small pie dishes for individual servings. Top the pie(s) with the mash and bake for around 15 minutes until golden.

Salt Fish and Ackee

Sandra (mum to Malachi Jempeji)

SERVES 4-6

Salt Fish and Ackee is Jamaica's national dish, and a favourite of ours as it's rich in flavour, but so quick to make. I used to help my mum make it when we had friends or family over for dinner as a child, and now I make it for my own family every Saturday evening. Ackee a yellow fruit with a buttery, creamy texture pairs beautifully with the salty cod.
This recipe, adapted from Cooking for Today: Caribbean Cooking by Jane Hartshorn, uses tinned ackee, which is much easier to handle than fresh (the skin, seeds and membrane of fresh ackee are poisonous, as is the flesh when unripe and overripe). Both salt cod and ackee can be found in the 'World Food' sections of major supermarkets, or in shops that sell West Indian produce. This dish is often eaten with fried plantain, but at home we serve it with basmati rice.

250G/8OZ SALT COD,
  SOAKED OVERNIGHT
30G/1OZ BUTTER
2 TABLESPOONS OLIVE OIL
2 SLICES STREAKY BACON, CHOPPED
4 SPRING ONIONS, SLICED
1 ONION, SLICED
1/2 TEASPOON DRIED THYME
2 FRESH GREEN CHILLIS, SLICED
  FINELY
1 GREEN PEPPER, SLICED
2 TOMATOES, SKINNED AND CHOPPED
350G/12 OZ CAN ACKEE, DRAINED
GROUND BLACK PEPPER, TO TASTE

Drain the salt cod and rinse under cold water. Put in a saucepan, cover with cold water and bring to the boil. Cover and simmer for 10 minutes. Drain, rinse, remove the skin and bones and flake the flesh. Heat the butter with the oil in a frying pan, add the bacon and fry for 5 minutes until crisp. Remove with a slotted spoon and place on a paper towel to absorb excess oil. Fry the spring onions, onion, thyme, chillies and pepper for 5 minutes. Add the tomatoes and cook for a further 5 minutes. Stir in the salt cod, ackee and bacon and cook for a further 2-3 minutes. Serve with fried plantains or rice.

Sweet Potato and Smoked Mackerel Jackets

Katherine (mum to Ariel Kellett)

SERVES 2

This recipe, given to me by my stepsister, is one I cook often, as it is so, so easy and so tasty.

2 SWEET POTATOES
2 SMOKED MACKEREL FILLETS, FLAKED
A BUNCH OF SPRING ONIONS, CHOPPED
A HANDFUL OF BLACK OLIVES (PITTED)
SPRINKLE OF DRIED CHILLI FLAKES
  (CAUTION - THESE ARE HOT!)

Cook the sweet potato either in the oven or the microwave. Five minutes before serving, put the smoked mackerel fillets in a pan and fry skin-side down until skin is crispy (you won't need any oil). Add the onions, olives and as many chilli flakes as you can handle to the pan, and heat for a further minute or two until the onion is soft. Split open the sweet potatoes and top with the mackerel mix. Serve with green leaves.

Salmon Oshi-sushi

Hiroko (mum to Kai and Mika McIsaac)

SERVES 4

Oshi-sushi (pressed sushi) is a great dish for those who adore sushi but have always thought it too complicated to make. It's also a thoughtful and delicious option for friends who are allergic to wheat. The key to the dish is getting the ingredients right. The rice must be short, fat Japanese rice (stickier than long grain rice) – look for 'sushi rice', available in most major supermarkets. Once the rice is cooked it needs seasoning: in Japan we use a powder called sushinoko, which we mix in with the cooked rice, but vinegar, sugar and salt do exactly the same job. However, the vinegar must be rice vinegar (often marketed as 'sushi vinegar') – no other type will do. When it comes to the fish, you can either choose sushi (sashimi) salmon from a good fishmonger (it must be extremely fresh, which rules out supermarket fish), or, if you are feeling less adventurous, you can use pre-packaged smoked salmon. If using raw salmon, allow a few hours for salting and marinating, and ask the fishmonger to slice it for you if you don't have a fish knife (Atariya near Norbiton station will do this). Oshi-sushi is made in a traditional wooden box called an oshibako with a lid, which compresses the rice and fish and makes it easy to cut into neat rectangles, but I usually use our late Aunt Bea's tart dish.

2 CUPS (360ML) SUSHI RICE

JUST OVER 2 CUPS (432ML) WATER – THE RATIO IS 1 (RICE): 1.2 (WATER)

50ML RICE VINEGAR, PLUS EXTRA FOR MARINATING (IF USING RAW SALMON)

12.5G CASTER SUGAR

5G SALT, PLUS EXTRA PINCH FOR SALTING (IF USING RAW SALMON)

500G SMOKED SALMON, OR EXTREMELY FRESH RAW SALMON (NOT FROM THE SUPERMARKET), SLICED THINLY (5-6MM)

"MY FAVOURITE FOOD IS SUSHI."

Nariman Diar

1-2 LEAVES OF FRESH SHISO-HERB OR FRESH CORIANDER, FINELY SLICED OR FINELY SLICED CUCUMBER (OPTIONAL)

SOY SAUCE AND WASABI PASTE, TO SERVE (OPTIONAL)

If using raw salmon, rub with a pinch of salt and leave in the fridge for up to two hours (although if you're in a hurry 30 minutes will be fine). Then cover with rice vinegar and leave for a further hour to marinate.

Place the rice in a pan with the water and leave to soak for 30 minutes. Bring to the boil then turn the heat right down and cook with the lid tightly on for about 30-45 minutes until the rice is thoroughly cooked and all the water has been absorbed. It's easier to use an electric rice cooker, if you have got one, but an ordinary pan is fine, although you must keep it covered – no peeking! To assess whether it is cooked or not, you need to smell it, rather than look under the lid (this is a skill that can be acquired through practise, although apparently the Japanese sense of smell is well recognised in the world – there are many excellent Japanese aromatherapists!). When the rice is cooked, spread it over a wide, flat bowl (we use a special dish called a sushi-oke) – this helps the rice cool down. Mix the vinegar, sugar and salt together and fold gently into the rice as if making a soufflé, without crushing the grains (you want the rice grains shiny and plump). Cover with a wet tea towel and leave to cool.

Line the bottom of a deep 18cm or 19cm tart dish or cake tin with cling film. Arrange the shiso-herb or coriander over the bottom of the tin. Sprinkle a few drops of rice vinegar over the smoked salmon if using, then place the smoked salmon or marinated raw salmon into the tin, over the sliced herb. Top with the rice, pressing it down to compact it (or you could top with half the rice, then layer over thinly-sliced cucumber followed by the remaining rice, like a Victoria sponge with jam). Cover with cling film and leave in a cool place with something heavy on the top (eg a plate and a few tins of beans) for about half an hour. Do not ever put it in the fridge as the rice becomes hard and inedible (just like supermarket sushi!). Turn out the sushi with the rice on the bottom and cut into slices (clean the knife between slices if rice gets stuck on the blade). Serve on a bamboo leaf on a plate, with soy sauce for dipping, wasabi paste and pickled ginger.

You know what they say about all work and no play... Time for some fun on the astro turf! These healthy snacks will restore energy levels after all that running around with eggs and spoons...

Post-match refreshments

Yummy Oat Biscuits

Senka (mum to Mischa and Bronte Escott)

MAKES APPROXIMATELY 12 LARGE BISCUITS

These biscuits are the absolute favourite in our house and we make them all the time. They are adapted from biscuits I came across in a yoga centre years ago. For the lunch box we omit nuts and for picnics and home snacks we make a slightly different version by combining different types of nuts, seeds and dried fruit. We especially like dried apricots with hazelnuts or walnuts. You can also vary the spices if you don't like what's on the list.

250G ROLLED OATS
100G WHOLEWHEAT FLOUR
120G BROWN SUGAR
100G NUTS OR SEEDS (CHOP NUTS INTO SMALL
    PIECES, BUT SEEDS CAN BE LEFT WHOLE)
100G DRIED FRUIT (CHOP APRICOTS INTO SMALL
    PIECES, BUT RAISINS ETC CAN BE LEFT WHOLE)
1 1/2 TEASPOON GROUND CINNAMON
1 1/2 TEASPOON GROUND GINGER
1 1/2 TEASPOON GRATED NUTMEG
1/2 TEASPOON BAKING POWDER
200ML OIL (SUNFLOWER OR COCONUT)
150-200ML WATER

Preheat the oven to 200°C/400°F/Gas Mark 6. Oil or line 1 or 2 baking sheets. Combine all the dry ingredients, add the oil and gradually add water until you make a firm mixture. Take a spoonful of mixture, roll it into a ball, place it onto a baking sheet and flatten. Bake for 11-14 minutes.

Fruit Bar

Laura (mum to Alfie Ward)

MAKES 12 SLICES

This recipe was passed to me by my friend's mum who was on a fat-free diet for health reasons. It has no fat, sugar (other than fructose in the fruit) or eggs and I have made it with gluten-free flour and it tasted lovely. It's also very quick and easy to throw together! You can vary the dried fruit, e.g. adding chopped dried cranberries, apricots or cherries.

```
250G STONED DATES
300ML WATER
175G SEEDLESS RAISINS
125G SULTANAS
125G CURRANTS
50G CANDIED MIXED PEEL, CHOPPED
175G WHOLEMEAL PLAIN FLOUR
3 TEASPOONS BAKING POWDER
1 TEASPOON MIXED SPICE
GRATED RIND AND JUICE OF
  1 ORANGE OR LEMON
25G GROUND ALMONDS
```

Preheat the oven to 160°C/325°F/Gas Mark 3. Line a 1kg/2lb tin or a 20cm/8in round tin with greaseproof paper. Place the dates in a saucepan with the measured water and heat gently until they are soft. Remove from the heat and mash with a fork until pureed. Place the date puree in a bowl with all the remaining ingredients and 4 tablespoons of water. Mix together well. Spoon the mixture into the prepared tin and level the top. Bake for 1½ hours until a skewer inserted in the middle comes out clean. Towards the end of the cooking you may need to protect the top of the cake with foil. Allow the cake to cool a little in the tin, then turn out and finish cooling on a wire rack.

But these slightly less healthy snacks might also be appreciated!

The Ultimate Choc-chip Cookie

Cadence (mum to Zaviana and Satya Lane)

MAKES 40-60

I am American, but my dad was born in Yorkshire, my mum in Lithuania, and my brother in Canada, so I am really the only American in my family! However, my cooking definitely has a strong American influence. This recipe is from the back of Nestlé Chocolate Chip bags in the USA. They have a complete corner in the market, and seem to be the only chocolate chips anyone buys, hence this has been a household recipe in the States for over 50 years. They are as classic an American staple as hot dogs, Coca Cola, and apple pie. The uncooked dough can be kept in the fridge for a week, or freezer for 8 weeks (divided into two 15in logs and wrapped in greaseproof paper).

2 1/4 CUPS PLAIN FLOUR
1 TEASPOON BICARBONATE OF SODA
1 TEASPOON SALT
1 CUP (225G) BUTTER, SOFTENED
3/4 CUP GRANULATED SUGAR
3/4 CUP PACKED (PRESSED DOWN FIRMLY IN THE CUP) LIGHT BROWN SUGAR
1 TEASPOON VANILLA EXTRACT
2 LARGE EGGS
2 CUPS CHOCOLATE CHIPS (I USE 3-4 100G TUBES OF A WELL-KNOWN SUPERMARKET'S CHOCOLATE CHUNKS, WHICH IS DEFINITELY MORE THAN 2 CUPS (!), BUT YOU CAN USE ANY CHOCOLATE YOU LIKE BROKEN INTO PIECES)
1 CUP CHOPPED NUTS (OPTIONAL)

Preheat the oven to 180°C/350°F/Gas Mark 4. Combine the flour, bicarbonate of soda and salt in a small bowl. Beat butter, granulated sugar, brown sugar and vanilla extract in large mixing bowl until creamy. Add the eggs, one at a time, beating well after each addition. Gradually beat in the flour mixture. Stir in the chocolate chips and nuts. Drop heaped tablespoons of the dough onto ungreased baking sheets and bake for 9-11 minutes or until golden brown. Cool on baking sheets for 2 minutes; remove to wire racks to cool completely.

Grandma Jo's Syrup Cake

Emma (mum to Alice and Sam Helbert)

MAKES ONE 8IN CAKE

My mum (Alice and Sam's Grandma Jo) used to make this every week as an after school treat for me and my brother and I now make it for my children. It is so easy, with no more than 10 minutes prep before bunging it in the oven for an hour. As it takes a while to cook, it is perfect to put in the oven before going to collect the kids from school and it's virtually ready by the time everyone is home. It's nice still slightly warm, but also good the next day.

12 OZ SELF-RAISING FLOUR
10 OZ GRANULATED SUGAR
2 TEASPOONS GROUND GINGER
4 OZ BUTTER
2 TABLESPOONS GOLDEN SYRUP
1 EGG
10FL OZ HOT WATER

Preheat the oven to 180°C/350°F/Gas Mark 4. Grease and line a deep 8" cake tin. Mix all the dry ingredients together until evenly blended, then rub in the butter until mixture resembles fine breadcrumbs (or pulse in a food processor). Mix syrup, egg and hot water together. Using a wooden spoon, stir this liquid into the flour mix until a smooth, soft batter is formed. Pour into the prepared tin. Bake on the middle shelf for about an hour, until a skewer inserted in the centre comes out clean. Turn out on to a wire rack to cool.

Good Old Bacon Butty

The Thurtell Family (Ross)

SERVES 1

There are always lots of hungry boys hanging out in our house. One of these (or two, if they've been running around lots!) keeps them very happy!

3 SLICES UNSMOKED OR
   SMOKED BACK BACON
   PER PERSON
2 SLICES OF SQUARE WHITE
   BREAD PER PERSON OR
   1 LARGE SOFT, WHITE BAP
GOOD QUALITY BUTTER
LARGE DOLLOP OF GOOD
   QUALITY TOMATO KETCHUP

Fry the bacon in a non-stick pan until it reaches the desired level of crispness. Meanwhile, spread one slice of the bread with butter and the other with ketchup, making sure each slice is completely covered. When the bacon is cooked to your liking, slip it onto the buttered slice, so the butter starts to melt. Top with the other slice and press down firmly. Cut into two, either from edge to edge, or, for a fancier butty, from corner to corner.

Coronation Chicken

Sue Bushnell (Taken from the first Bishop Gilpin cookbook, edited by Barbara Zarzycki and Rose Williams, July 2002).

SERVES 6

This is a cheat's version of the more time-consuming classic recipe, which calls for a home-made curry base. All quantities are approximate – the strength of the sauce is a matter of personal preference!

6 CHICKEN BREASTS
1 MEDIUM JAR OF GOOD
  QUALITY MAYONNAISE
1 SMALL TUB SOUR CREAM
2 TABLESPOONS GOOD
  QUALITY CURRY PASTE
1 TABLESPOON MANGO
  CHUTNEY
2 TEASPOONS TOMATO PUREE
SPLASH LEMON JUICE
2 HANDFULS DRIED
  APRICOTS, CUT INTO
  STRIPS
1 FEW SULTANAS
SALT AND PEPPER, TO TASTE

Roast the chicken in the oven until just cooked – it should be cooked through but still moist and tender. Cut into fork-sized chunks when cool. Mix together the other ingredients and combine with the cooled chicken.

Wimbledon Cake

Elizabeth Broad (Taken from the first Bishop Gilpin cookbook, edited by Barbara Zarzycki and Rose Williams, July 2002).

MAKES ONE 7 X 11 IN TRAY BAKE

This recipe was used for at least 20 years on St Mary's picnic stall during Tennis Fortnight, and has fed literally thousands of hungry tennis fans over the years. It's absolutely delicious! As it contains fresh apples it doesn't keep well, so either eat up immediately or store in the fridge.

8OZ SELF-RAISING FLOUR
4OZ GRANULATED SUGAR
1 EGG, BEATEN IN A LITTLE MILK
4OZ BUTTER OR MARGARINE
1OOZ APPLES, PEELED, CORED AND
DICED (2-3 MEDIUM APPLES)

Preheat the oven to 180°C/350°F/Gas Mark 4. Grease a 7 x 11 inch cake tin. Rub fat into flour. Add sugar and apple, then mix in the egg and milk. Bake for approximately 40 minutes, or until a skewer inserted in the centre comes out clean.

Quick Strawberry Ice Cream

Simon from Riverford Organic Farms (dad to Alex Harrop)

SERVES 4

This recipe, taken from the Riverford Organic Farms website (www.riverford.co.uk), is very easy to make at home as it doesn't require an ice cream machine. The addition of alcohol helps the freezing process, but feel free to leave it out. Choose very ripe strawberries for the best flavour.

500G STRAWBERRIES
1 TABLESPOON ORANGE JUICE
2 TABLESPOONS HONEY
5OML RED WINE (OPTIONAL)
2OOML DOUBLE CREAM
150G PLAIN YOGHURT

Whizz the strawberries, orange juice, honey and red wine in a food processor, then strain through a fine sieve to remove the seeds. Whip the double cream and yoghurt together until they form soft peaks, then fold them into the strawberry purée. Freeze until firm. About 20 minutes before serving, transfer to the fridge to soften slightly.

lunch boxes and picnics

Bored of white bread and processed ham sandwiches? Our Japanese families have some great ideas for cool lunch-boxes which will tempt even the fussiest of eaters...

Japanese Lunch Boxes (Obento)

Interview with Hiroko McIsaac, Kyoko Boheringer, Miki Miyasaka, Mayumi Ishiguro, Satomi Mearashi

Obento is a special kind of Japanese lunch, for eating out of the home: on trains, school or university excursions, or even during the interval at the theatre. It's carried around in boxes that come in all sorts of different colours, shapes and sizes. In Japan, the food inside the box is as colourful as the outside, and preparing obento has been elevated to an art form.

There are a few rules that must be followed in order to make a good obento. First and foremost, the food should please the eye as much as the palate. The contents of the box should be bright, and the presentation imaginative: food is typically formed into shapes such as flowers, stars, animals or even well-known cartoon characters! Walk into any Japanese supermarket and you will be able to buy all sorts of tools and special foods to help with this task: dainty cutters; punches for making holes in nori seaweed; moulds for shaping rice (eg pandas); special pans for rolling omelettes into rectangles; pre-cut nori (seaweed) shapes (Pokemon is popular for children!); dyed shiso (a dried herb). Secondly, as well as satisfying the taste buds, obento must be balanced nutritionally. This is usually achieved by following the principle of serving something from the sea (eg fish, crustaceans, seaweed), from the mountain (eg root vegetables, mushrooms, nuts), from the ground (eg beef, pork, chicken) and the main staple, the rice.

When the cookbook team gasped at the amount of effort involved, we reminded them of the work that goes into the British craze of baking, and the money spent on baking paraphernalia: different shaped tins; colourful cake cases; weird and wonderful toppings. And we don't go to town every day: it's actually possible to rustle up a beautiful obento fairly quickly by using the leftovers from last night's evening meal (children and adults eat the same food, which makes life easier). Also, we make good use of tinned foods and the freezer, often freezing small portions of leftovers just for obento. Of course, for special occasions – school picnics or sports days, for example - a lot more time goes into the process. Its not unknown for some mums to spend several hours crafting a masterpiece, especially when they know other mothers will be watching and comparing!

summer term 157

Japanese people are like magpies – when we move to a foreign country we don't just stick to the traditional foods of Japan, we rummage through freezer cabinets, market stalls and grocery aisles to find new foods to which we can apply our principles of presentation. Happy discoveries in the UK include frozen okra (sliced thinly it makes beautiful star shapes), German-style frankfurter sausages and Serrano ham (great wrapped around asparagus). And for ingredients like sushi rice, shiso herb, teriyaki smoked eel and nori we have local stores such as Ataria in Norbiton or Korea Food in New Malden. Anyone can make a good obento – all you need is imagination!

"ANYONE CAN MAKE A GOOD OBENTO — ALL YOU NEED IS IMAGINATION!"

summer term 139

Tanya's Chicken Goujons

Deborah (mum to Marcus and Pia)

SERVES 4

This recipe – from our dear friend Tanya – is one of my children's favourite meals. The yoghurt means the goujons don't dry out and the garlic gives them a delicious flavour. I have yet to find a child who doesn't like them! Also good for picnics.

3 LARGE CHICKEN BREASTS, CUT INTO STRIPS
700G NATURAL OR GREEK YOGHURT
3-4 GARLIC CLOVES, CRUSHED
200G BREADCRUMBS
SALT AND PEPPER

Preheat the oven to 180°C/350°F/Gas Mark 4. Lightly oil a baking tray. Place chicken, yoghurt, garlic and seasoning in a bowl and stir gently until well mixed. Cover and leave in fridge to marinate (I usually leave for 3 hours but anything over an hour should be fine). Pour breadcrumbs into a bowl and roll marinated chicken pieces in the crumbs until thoroughly coated. Place on baking tray, and cook for around 30 minutes, turning after 10 minutes, until golden brown on the outside and piping hot on the inside. Delicious with home-made potato wedges, vegetables and a dollop of tomato ketchup.

Quesadillas

Nicola (mum to Emily and Jessica Downer)

SERVES 4-6

Katie, our lovely au-pair, learned this recipe from Mexican friends when she was previously living with another family in Colorado, USA. We all love it when she makes it and the children enjoy helping with the cooking.

FOUR CHICKEN BREASTS OR BONELESS THIGHS, CHOPPED INTO CHUNKS
1 TEASPOON PAPRIKA
1/2 TEASPOON MILD CHILLI POWDER (OR MORE FOR ADULTS!)
PINCH OF SALT AND PEPPER
1 TEASPOON OLIVE OIL, PLUS EXTRA FOR FRYING
1 RED ONION, SLICED
1 RED PEPPER, SLICED
1 GREEN PEPPER, SLICED
GRATED CHEESE, ENOUGH FOR A HANDFUL PER PERSON
4-6 LARGE FLOUR TORTILLAS (ONE PER PERSON)

Mix the chicken with the paprika, chilli powder, salt and pepper. Stir in the oil and leave to marinate in the fridge for 30 minutes (if you have time!). Fry the chicken in a non-stick pan until cooked through and piping hot in the middle, transfer to a clean bowl and keep warm with foil over the top. Fry the onions and peppers until tender but still with a little bite, and add to the chicken. Cook the tortillas one at a time in a non-stick pan, adding a little oil if necessary. Add some of the chicken and peppers to half of the tortilla and sprinkle with cheese. Fold the other half of the tortilla over, and cook gently, turning once, until both sides look golden and the cheese has melted. Cut into two and serve immediately, with warm rice. Carry on making more!

Gingerbread Men

Alex Sherratt

MAKES ABOUT 8

This is my award-winning recipe as I won first prize for my gingerbread men at the school summer fair in 2012. I love making them as it's lots of fun decorating them and giving them silly outfits – they are also yummy to eat!

170G BUTTER, SOFTENED
85G BROWN SUGAR
200G PLAIN FLOUR
2 TEASPOONS GROUND GINGER
2 TEASPOONS CINNAMON
FINELY GRATED ZEST OF 1 ORANGE
COLOURED ICING PENS, TO DECORATE

Preheat the oven to 190°C/375°F/Gas Mark 5. Cream the butter and sugar together with a wooden spoon in a large bowl until light and fluffy (you can use an electric mixer, but I like doing it by hand). Add all the other ingredients and mix them together. Squeeze the mixture into a ball with your hands. Wrap the ball in a plastic bag and put in the fridge for 2 hours. Roll out the dough to 5mm thick. Remember to sprinkle some flour on the table to stop the dough from sticking. Use your gingerbread man shape to cut out the figures. Place the men on a non-stick baking tray. Bake them in the oven for 15 minutes. Remove them from the oven and put them on a rack to cool. When the biscuits are cold, decorate them with icing pens.

Robin's Chocolate Apricots

Robin Blair

MAKES 20

This recipe is my invention but other people may have thought of it too. You can use any small pieces of fruit as long as the surface is dry. Orange segments are nice but be careful the stick does not slip out! I prefer milk chocolate but some people prefer dark chocolate. You can roll the chocolate-coated fruit in sprinkles before the chocolate sets if you like.

200G DARK OR MILK
  CHOCOLATE
20 DRIED APRICOTS
COCKTAIL STICKS

Put a cocktail stick in each piece of fruit. Line a baking tray with greaseproof paper. Melt the chocolate slowly in a pan over a gentle heat. Stir it until there are no lumps of chocolate left. Top tip: you must stir it all the time or it will boil. Remove from the heat. Dip each apricot in the pan until lightly covered with melted chocolate. Twizzle the stick over the pan to make sure that the chocolate isn't too thick because it will be too rich. Carefully place each stick on the baking paper. You need to coat the fruit quite quickly before the chocolate starts to thicken again. When they are all on the tray leave them to set in a cool place. If you put them in the fridge it is quicker.

Or maybe this is ore your style?!

The first time I made this curry was for a picnic at an open-air concert. I needed to feed lots of hungry family members, and the usual cold collation would have been quite expensive as well as cumbersome to transport. By providing a Thai green curry we had only to carry a large cooking pot, a container of rice and the crockery and cutlery. When I opened the lid of the pot with the curry, its fabulous exotic aroma infused the night air, eliciting levels of picnic-envy from concert-goers up to 40 yards away, making ours all the more delicious! I hope you will now enjoy this recipe as much as we all have.

Thai Green Chicken Curry

Edward (dad to Nelly Boydell)

SERVES 4

1 TABLESPOON VEGETABLE OIL
3 TEASPOONS THAI GREEN CURRY PASTE
   (AVAILABLE IN ANY SUPERMARKET)
400G CHICKEN BREAST, CUT INTO
   LARGE-ISH CUBES
400ML COCONUT MILK
2 TEASPOONS THAI FISH SAUCE
100G GREEN BEANS, TOPPED, TAILED
   AND CUT INTO 2CM PIECES
3 DRIED KAFFIR LIME LEAVES,
   CRUMBLED
225G BAMBOO SHOOTS
LEAVES FROM 1 PACK OF FRESH
   BASIL, ROUGHLY TORN

Heat the oil with the curry paste in a large pan for about a minute and then stir in the chicken, and fry it for about five minutes turning it constantly until it is just cooked. Add the coconut milk, the fish sauce, the green beans and the lime leaves. Cover the pan and simmer for 10-12 minutes, until chicken is cooked through and piping hot inside. Add the bamboo shoots, simmer for 2 minutes then add the basil and simmer for 2 further minutes.
Serve with fragrant Thai rice.

Summer parties

Whether marking exam success, a birthday or anniversary or the end of an era, here are some summer crowd pleasers. Let's Fiesta!

Catalan Paella

The Coursey family (Audrey and Kate)

SERVES 4

Paella and its different rice and pasta variations (dishes with a base of fish stock, shellfish and meat, such as fideus, arrossejat and arròs negre) was born in the Països Catalans, the Catalan-speaking coastal regions of the west coast of Spain. Each town along the Països Catalans – which extends from Cataluniya in the North all the way down to Valencia in the South – has its own version, based on what the fisherman have brought to port that day! During the summer in Barcelona we cook it on the open fire in the garden every Saturday, the day when we congregate with family and friends, to celebrate being free from work and to indulge in good food, good wine and each others' company. Each week a different member of the family or friend will cook it, so it gets quite competitive! In England we make paella every time we have people over – it's a great dish for sharing and for marking a sense of occasion. Also once a month I cook it instead of a roast (Audrey's request)! The kids love it and they have understood from a very young age the importance of getting together and sharing food as a way of life.

NB It's easy to chop the meat yourself, but the butcher will do it for you if you haven't got the right knife. I order langoustines in advance from the fish counter of my local supermarket (where I can also buy fresh baby squid), but feel free to use extra prawns instead if you can't get hold of any. The freezer section of the supermarket is a good place to look for fish, eg frozen prepared squid (just defrost and dry with kitchen towel). You will need a paella pan or pan wide enough so that the rice is no more than three fingers deep whilst cooking.

"PAELLA HAS A SWEET TANGY FLAVOUR THAT MAKES YOUR MOUTH WATER THINKING ABOUT IT. THE PRAWNS ARE ONE THING BUT WITH THE RICE AND SAUCE AND VEGETABLES, ITS LIKE HEAVEN AND PARADISE PUT TOGETHER."

Eliza King-Christopher

8 MUSSELS
A HANDFUL OF CLAMS
3-4 TABLESPOONS OLIVE OIL
350G BOMBA (PAELLA) RICE
200G CHICKEN THIGHS ON THE
    BONE, EACH CHOPPED IN TWO
200G PORK RIBS, EACH RIB
    CHOPPED INTO 3 PIECES
4 RAW WHOLE KING PRAWNS
    (SHELL ON)
4 WHOLE LANGOUSTINES
    (SHELL ON)
SEA SALT
200G CALAMARI, CLEANED
    AND CUT INTO LITTLE PIECES
    (OR BABY SQUID, CLEANED
    AND TENTACLES REMOVED)
100G FROZEN PETITS POIS
1 LITRE FRESH FISH STOCK,
    HEATED TO BOILING POINT

FOR THE SOFRITO
1 MEDIUM ONION, FINELY CHOPPED
1/2 RED PEPPER, FINELY CHOPPED
1/2 GREEN PEPPER, FINELY
    CHOPPED
2 TOMATOES, GRATED (SKIN AND
    PIPS REMOVED)
1 1/2 GARLIC CLOVES, CRUSHED
FOR THE PICADA
A HANDFUL OF PARSLEY
1/2 GARLIC CLOVE
GENEROUS PINCH OF SAFFRON
    (ONE SMALL BOX)

Scrub the mussels in a sinkful of cold water, pull out the beards from between the tightly closed shells and scrape off any barnacles with a knife. Discard any that are broken or any open ones that won't close tightly when tapped with a knife. Give the mussels a final rinse to remove any last pieces of grit or shell. Wash the clams thoroughly under running water, discarding any that are broken or any open ones that won't close tightly when tapped with a knife. Heat the olive oil in a paella pan or large wide pan. Sprinkle sea salt over the ribs and chicken pieces then brown over a high heat. Set aside, keeping the oil. Sprinkle salt over the prawns and langoustines then sear over a high heat and set aside. Do not discard the oil as it is needed for the sofrito.

To prepare the sofrito (ie the paste that forms the base of many Spanish stews and soups) cook the onion and peppers in the oil in which the meat and fish were seared on the lowest heat for a good 20 minutes or so until soft and sweet, stirring regularly, then add the garlic and tomatoes and cook for a further 5 or 10 minutes. When the sofrito is starting to caramelise, turn the heat up high and add the calamari. Sear for about a minute (no longer, to avoid overcooking) then add the rice and cook for a few minutes, stirring thoroughly so that all the grains are coated (this will make the rice really tasty). Before the rice starts to brown, add the reserved fried meats, the cleaned mussels and clams, the peas and the boiling stock. Stir and taste for salt, adding extra if necessary. Make the picada (ie a seasoning added to flavour the dish) by bashing the garlic, parsley and saffron in a pestle and mortar until paste-like. Mix in a tablespoon of water then pour the picada over the bubbling paella. Turn the heat down and cook for 15 minutes. Do not cover and do not stir the rice. Bon profit!

Colombian Empanadas

Carolina (nanny to Olivia and Charlie Graham)

MAKES APPROXIMATELY 20

I am proud of the cuisine in Colombia and love giving it to people from other countries so they can taste a little bit of my culture. Colombian empanadas are one of the most popular snacks in my country. They're perfect for parties or barbecues and one is just not enough, as some of the mums at school who have tried them will confirm! I buy masarepa (pre-cooked cornmeal) in the Latin American markets in Brixton or Elephant and Castle, but it can be found in some of the Asian stalls in Tooting market as well. Some of the supermarkets sell a fine-milled polenta flour (eg Natco fine cornmeal), which makes an acceptable substitute (although not as yellow!) Serve with hot spicy sauce (aji), wedges of lemon or lime and guacamole.

DOUGH:
3 CUPS PRE-COOKED YELLOW
    CORNMEAL (MASAREPA)
1/2 TEASPOON GARLIC GRANULES
1/2 TABLESPOON SAFFRON
1/2 TEASPOON CUMIN
PINCH OF SALT
2 CUPS WATER
JUICE OF 1 LEMON

FILLING:
1 TABLESPOON OLIVE OIL
1 ONION, FINELY DICED
    OR GRATED
1 BEEF STOCK CUBE
2 TOMATOES, FINELY DICED
1 CLOVE OF GARLIC, CRUSHED
1 TABLESPOON PAPRIKA
1/2 TABLESPOON SAFFRON
1/2 TEASPOON CUMIN
1/2LB STEWING BEEF,
    CUT INTO 1CM CUBES
2 POTATOES, PEELED AND DICED

VEGETABLE OIL,
    FOR DEEP-FRYING
PINCH OF SALT AND PEPPER

First, make the dough by placing the cornmeal, garlic granules, saffron, cumin and salt in a bowl and stirring to mix well. Stir in the water and lemon juice then, using your hands, bring together into a ball. Knead for about 5 minutes until the dough is smooth, pat into a ball, place in a freezer bag and set aside.

To make the filling, heat the olive oil in a pan. Add the onion, crumble in the stock cube and fry until the onion is soft. Add the tomatoes, garlic, paprika, saffron and cumin and cook for a further 8 to 10 minutes, stirring frequently. Add the beef and the salt and pepper, and cook until tender (about one hour). Leave to cool. Meanwhile, boil the potatoes until tender. Drain and crush lightly with a potato masher, so that there are still chunky pieces. When cooled, mix thoroughly with the beef mixture.

When you are ready to make the empanadas, take a small portion of the dough (about 1 big tablespoon) and roll into a small ball. Place between two pieces of cling film and roll into a circle, about 4in in diameter. Remove the top piece of cling film and place a tablespoon of the beef mix in the centre. Using the bottom piece of cling film, fold the dough over the filling to enclose it, then seal the edges (I always use a cup to do this but you can also pinch round the edges). Repeat until all the dough is used up. Heat 2-3 inches oil in a deep, heavy pan on a medium high-heat until hot enough to deep-fry (170-190°C or 350-375°F, or hot enough that a cube of bread dropped in browns in 60 seconds). Fry in batches until the outside is crisp and golden and the filling is piping hot, about 3-4 minutes per batch. Remove with a slotted spoon and drain on paper towels before serving warm. Y listo!

"EMPANADAS ARE ONE OF THE MOST POPULAR SNACKS IN MY COUNTRY.
THEY'RE PERFECT FOR PARTIES OR BARBECUES AND ONE IS JUST NOT ENOUGH."

Guacamole

Carolina (nanny to Olivia and Charlie Graham)

SERVES 4-6

2 RIPE AVOCADOS
1 ONION, FINELY SLICED
1 TOMATO, FINELY CHOPPED
1 CLOVE OF GARLIC, FINELY CHOPPED
1 RED CHILLI, FINELY CHOPPED (SEEDS REMOVED)
1 TABLESPOON OLIVE OIL
3 TABLESPOONS FINELY CHOPPED CORIANDER
JUICE OF 1 LEMON
SALT AND PEPPER

Remove the stones from the avocados, setting one aside. Place the avocados
in a bowl and roughly mash with a fork or potato masher (remember it has to
look chunky). Gently mix in the remaining ingredients, reserving a handful
of the coriander for decoration. Place an avocado stone in the middle of the
guacamole to help keep it fresh for longer, and sprinkle with the rest of the
coriander. y listo a disfrutar!

BY LARA

This is Christian's great granny's version of a classic Persian lamb dish and is lovely to cook when broad beans are in season (but works equally well with frozen broad beans, a supermarket staple). This can also be served as a vegetarian dish (obviously without the meat!). There are many variations of this recipe: you can use chicken instead of lamb, and some people add a little cinnamon to the stock and fried onions to the rice but our way is very tasty without too much prep! The lamb can be cooked in advance and reheated before serving.

Baghalli Polo Ba Goosht (Rice and Broad Beans with Lamb)

Afsana (mum to Christian Short)

SERVES 4-6

FOR THE LAMB STEW:
1.5KG LAMB NECK FILLET,
  CUT INTO LARGE CUBES
  (APPROXIMATELY 5CM), OR
  LEG OF LAMB ON THE BONE
1.5L WATER, OR ENOUGH
  TO COVER THE MEAT
2 LARGE ONIONS, PEELED
  AND QUARTERED
1 MEDIUM BULB GARLIC,
  PEELED
1 TEASPOON TURMERIC
1 TEASPOON SALT
1/2 TEASPOON FINE GROUND
  WHITE PEPPER

FOR THE RICE:
1 1/2 CUPS BASMATI RICE
1KG FRESH BROAD BEANS (OR
  FROZEN BEANS, DEFROSTED)
1 LEVEL TABLESPOON SALT
1-2 LARGE, THIN SOFT FLAT
  BREADS (OR SEVERAL
  LARGE LETTUCE LEAVES,
  WASHED AND DRIED)
1 TABLESPOONS VEGETABLE
  OIL
1 TABLESPOON BUTTER
1/2 CUP DRIED DILL OR
  CHOPPED FRESH DILL

TO SERVE:
50G BUTTER, MELTED
1 TEASPOON SAFFRON
  THREADS
GREEK YOGHURT

Place lamb in a saucepan with the onion, garlic, turmeric, salt and pepper and cover with water. Including the bone will create a more flavoursome stock. Bring to the boil then turn the heat down and simmer with the lid on for 1½-2 hours, until the meat is tender/ falls off the bone. You want to end up with about a cup of liquid, so check contents of pan occasionally and adjust levels accordingly (ie add more water if evaporating too fast or remove lid and reduce liquid if looking too watery). Set aside meat (removing meat from bone if necessary) along with the stock and soft onions. Discard the bone and some of the garlic (if desired – we like it garlicky!). If using fresh broad beans boil until tender, cool under running water then drain and pop them out of their skins (if using frozen beans no need to boil – just defrost before skinning). Set aside. Bring a half-filled saucepan of water to the boil, add the rice, beans and salt and heat on high for 3-4 minutes until the water comes back to the boil. Stirring very occasionally, let boil for a further 2 minutes until the rice grows in length and is al dente but not cooked. Drain the rice and the beans (taste for salt and adjust accordingly).

Place the vegetable oil and butter in a large saucepan and heat gently until warm. Remove from the heat and distribute the flatbread or lettuce evenly over the oily base. Put a layer of rice and beans over the pitta then sprinkle over a layer of dill; repeat until all the rice and dill are used up then sprinkle over ¼ cup cold water. (This will steam the rice) Put the pan back on the stove, cover with a clean tea towel then push the lid firmly over the pot – this is very important and ensures that the steam is locked inside. Cook for 30 minutes on a medium heat, without opening the lid. The rice is ready when there is plenty of steam in the upper part of the pot (this is easier to judge if you have a see-through lid!). To finish the dish, pour the melted butter all over the rice in the saucepan, then gently arrange the rice and beans on a large dish and serve with the lamb stew on the top. Mix the saffron with 2-3 tablespoons of hot water and stir into some of the rice as a garnish. Finally, arrange the flatbread/ lettuce crust (this is known as the 'tahdig') on the top. It looks slightly burnt but don't worry – it will add a sweet bitter flavour (which is suprisingly delicious!). A trick to get the tahdig out is to place the hot pan into a sink of very cold water so the pan contracts and releases the yummy bottom! Serve with thick Greek-style yoghurt.

This is an old Sophie Grigson recipe that lists garlic as an ingredient.
I used to use garlic until a Spanish friend was outraged at this completely
unnecessary addition. I usually serve this hot, when we're having lots of family
for lunch, with a large range of tastes. My very fussy teenage nephew can be
bribed to come and visit us if he knows it's on the menu! The plate sporting
the tortilla will often be held up on its way round the table as my family try
to help themselves to larger than polite pieces of this delicious 'omelette.'
It might seem like a time-wasting fuss for a mere omelette but, be warned, this
is no ordinary omelette!

Family Favourite Tortilla

Christobel (mum to Nelly Boydell)

SERVES 4 AS A MAIN COURSE OR 8 AS A SNACK

OLIVE OIL
SUNFLOWER OIL
3 MEDIUM-SIZED POTATOES, PEELED AND THINLY SLICED
1 ONION, THINLY SLICED
8 EGGS, LIGHTLY BEATEN
SALT AND PEPPER

Pour a thin layer of olive oil into a wide, heavy-based frying pan (preferably one with a lid).
Pile in all the potatoes and onion then pour over enough oil to cover the mixture. Use a mix
of olive and sunflower oil. Cover with a lid and stew very gently, over a low flame, until the
vegetables are tender. Allow at least half an hour for this. The potato and onion should be
meltingly tender but not brown. Lift out with a slotted spoon and place on kitchen paper to
absorb excess oil, reserving the cooking oil for later.

Season the eggs and add the potato mixture to the bowl. Leave for 15-30 minutes. Heat 3
tablespoons of the oil used for stewing the potatoes in a 23-30 cm (9-12in) frying pan over a
medium heat. Tip in the egg and potato mixture and smooth down. Cook until three-quarters
set. The sides should be a rich brown when eased from the pan. Finish by browning under
the grill. Check that the tortilla is just set through but still moist. Cool for a few minutes in the
pan (if your braying family will allow!), then turn out onto a plate.

BY HERBIE

The recipe comes via a family friend in South Africa as butternut is a very popular vegetable in South Africa. The recipe is great if you have offered to bring a salad to a barbecue but have run out of inspiration and a packet of salad leaves from the supermarket is not enough!

Butternut Feta Salad

The Coppin family (Caitlyn, Michael and Lauryn)

SERVES 6-8

2 BUTTERNUT SQUASH,
  PEELED, DESEEDED AND
  CUT INTO 2CM CHUNKS
  (OR CHEAT AND USE THE
  PRE-PREPARED PACKS -
  - I USUALLY USE 3
  PACKS)
1 TABLESPOON OLIVE OIL
50G SEED MIX (MY LOCAL
  SUPERMARKET HAS A GREAT
  ONE HELPFULLY CALLED
  'SEED MIX' - FOUND IN
  THE BAKING AISLE)
200G FETA CHEESE
2 GENEROUS HANDFULS OF
  ROCKET (YOU COULD USE
  BABY SPINACH IF ROCKET
  IS TOO PEPPERY FOR YOUR
  TASTE)

DRESSING:
3 TABLESPOONS OLIVE OIL
1 TABLESPOON BALSAMIC
  VINEGAR

Preheat the oven to 200°C/400°F/Gas Mark 6. Put the cubes of squash in a roasting tin, trickle over the oil and toss to coat. Roast for approximately 25 minutes until softened and starting to caramelise slightly round the edges. While the squash is roasting toast the seeds. Warm a heavy-bottomed frying pan over a medium heat, toast the seeds for a minute, constantly moving the pan so they toast evenly and don't burn. Arrange the roasted squash in a serving dish and crumble the feta over the squash while still warm. Mix in the seeds. Just before serving, whisk together the olive oil and balsamic vinegar, pour over the squash and feta and toss in the rocket.

"IF I COULD CHOOSE A MEAL ON MY BIRTHDAY IT WOULD BE A BARBECUE WITH BREAD, SALAD, CHOPS, SAUSAGES, AND A MASSIVE WEDDING CAKE - ONE LAYER CHOCOLATE, ONE BLUE VELVET CAKE AND ANOTHER LAYER VICTORIA SPONGE."

Poppy Reed

Mandy's Magnificent Mielie Bake

Paula (mum to Daniel Buchel)

This South African bake – made from the coarse, white cornmeal known as mielie – is a little similar to polenta, but so much more delicious. It is a great wheat-free carbohydrate and an ideal accompaniment to a barbecue, or braai. It is not only a summer food though, as it could be used in the place of a potato bake at any time. Daniel's aunt in South Africa passed on this recipe and it has become a favourite in our household. I always make extra to heat up the next day (if there is any left over!). The tinned sweetcorn and mielie meal can be bought at some supermarkets that stock South African products, or at your local SA shop. (Do not try and substitute with other products I have tried and it just wasn't the same). It is exceptionally easy and quick to make, and will surprise you how yummy it is.

4 EGGS
6 HEAPED TABLESPOONS
  MIELIE MEAL
2 TINS OF CREAMED
  SWEETCORN (SOUTH AFRICAN)
4 TEASPOONS BAKING POWDER
LARGE PINCH SALT
500ML CREAM

Preheat the oven to 180°C/350°F/Gas Mark 4. Lightly grease an oven-proof dish or tin (when the mixture is in it needs to be 3-5cm deep). Lightly beat the eggs and put to one side. Place the remaining ingredients in the dish and stir well to combine. Add the eggs and mix well. Bake for 45-60 minutes, until a skewer inserted in the centre comes out clean. Cut into large squares and serve hot.

Shashlik

The Harin family (Nikolai and Sophia)

As a South African/Russian family we tend to barbecue a lot in summer (and even sporadically in winter!). In South Africa a barbecue (or braai – pronounced 'br-eye') tends to be a social affair and will often take the form of a 'bring-and-braai' where the guests bring along a salad or meat to be barbecued. Popular choices include various cuts of meat, boerewors (a beef and pork sausage) and sosaties (kebabs). In our household we tend to buy the sosaties from the South African butcher, but more often, we tend to make Russian shashlik. Although it's probably more a middle-eastern dish, it is very popular in Russia, and because the meat is grilled on skewers, these are perfect to make over an open fire at your dacha (summer house). In Russia shashlik are made using flat metal skewers called shampuri, which help the meat cook from inside, but normal bamboo kebab skewers should work too (soaked in water so the protruding ends don't burn straight away).

MAKES 4-5 SKEWERS (SERVES
4 PEOPLE WITH SALADS ETC)

1LB LAMB (NECK, SHOULDER
  OR FATTIER CUTS, SO
  THAT THE MEAT DOES NOT
  BECOME DRY) OR PORK, CUT
  INTO BITE-SIZED CHUNKS
3 OR 4 LARGE ONIONS,
  CHOPPED ROUGHLY (YOU
  CAN'T GO WRONG WITH TOO
  MUCH ONION HERE!)
2 TABLESPOONS APPLE CIDER
  VINEGAR
1 TEASPOON SALT
BLACK PEPPER
3 BAY LEAVES
LARGE HANDFUL OF CORIANDER
  LEAVES, ROUGHLY CHOPPED
HALF A BUNCH OF SPRING
  ONIONS, FINELY SLICED

Place meat, onions, vinegar, bay leaves and a generous amount of black pepper in a container and mix well. Seal and refrigerate overnight. If you like you can mix the meat again after a few hours to redistribute the on-ions. When you are ready to cook the meat, mix the salt into the mixture, push the meat onto the skewers (discarding the onions) and barbecue over the hot coals, taking care not to overcook. Finally, serve with a gener-ous sprinkling of coriander and spring onions. In Russia shashlik is also often eaten with adjika (a slightly spicy tomato-based paste), but you can achieve a very similar effect with spicy or normal ketchup.

Bulgogi (Korean Barbecue)

The Shin family (Eugene)

SERVES 4

Bulgogi means 'fire meat' in Korean, and is one of Korea's most famous dishes. It's very thinly sliced beef, typically sirloin, which is marinated and then cooked over a flame. Nowadays we tend to cook it indoors in a frying pan, but it would work really well on an outdoor barbecue (if you line the grill with foil so the small pieces don't fall through). We often buy bulgogi pre-sliced from Korean supermarkets, but you can do it at home (it's easier if you firm up the meat in the freezer first). Asian pears (nashi) tenderise the meat and add a natural sweetness. Kiwi makes a good substitute. We usually wrap bulgogi in a lettuce leaf and eat with chopsticks, accompanied by sticky rice, ssamjang (hot sauce) and kimchi (fermented vegetables).

```
300G BEEF SIRLOIN
1 ONION, CUT INTO 0.5CM SLICES

MARINADE:
2 TABLESPOONS SOY SAUCE
1 TABLESPOON SESAME OIL
1 TABLESPOON SUGAR
1/2 TABLESPOON HONEY
1 TABLESPOON CRUSHED GARLIC
1/2 TABLESPOON CRUSHED SESAME SEEDS
A DASH OF GROUND BLACK PEPPER
50G PEELED AND PUREED ASIAN (NASHI) PEAR,
   OR 50G PEELED AND PUREED KIWI (OPTIONAL)
```

Rinse beef thoroughly under running water then pat dry with kitchen towel. Trim off gristle or fat using scissors, and cut across the grain into paper-thin slices, about 1-2mm thick (this is easier if the beef is partially frozen). Put all the marinade ingredients in a bowl and mix. Put the beef, onion and marinade into a large bowl and mix well to ensure each slice is coated. Leave to marinate for a minimum of 30 minutes (overnight is even better!). When you are ready to cook, heat griddle or pan until meat sizzles when it touches the pan. Drain off marinade and cook bulgogi and onions on high heat for 7-10 minutes until the edges of the bulgogi are brown and crispy.

Niamh's Moist Chocolate Loaf Cake

The Park family (Niamh)

MAKES TWO 10 IN LOAVES, OR ONE LARGE TRAYBAKE

Niamh's grandma, who lives in Australia, made this lovely light moist chocolate cake for Niamh's mummy when she was a girl. It's a family favourite and we often make it for birthdays, covered with hundreds of Smarties.

4OZ BUTTER, SOFTENED
2 CUPS CASTER SUGAR (250ML)
2 EGGS, LIGHTLY BEATEN
2 DESSERTSPOONS GOLDEN SYRUP (10ML)
3 CUPS SELF-RAISING FLOUR, SIFTED
4 HEAPED DESSERTSPOONS COCOA POWDER, SIFTED
1 CUP MILK
1 TEASPOON VANILLA ESSENCE
1 TEASPOON BICARBONATE OF SODA
1 CUP OF BOILING WATER

Preheat the oven to 180°C/350°F/Gas Mark 4. Grease and line two 10in/26cm loaf tins, or one large roasting tin (12 x 9 x 1½in /30 x 23 x 4cm). Cream the butter and sugar together with an electric mixer, until light and fluffy. Then add the eggs followed by the golden syrup. Sift the flour and cocoa together and fold in, a little at a time, alternating with spoonfuls of the milk. Stir the bicarbonate of soda into the boiling water then add to the mixture along with the vanilla and stir gently until smooth. Pour into tins and bake for approximately 30 minutes, until a skewer inserted into the centre comes out clean. Ice with lots of thick chocolate icing before serving.

"CHOCOLATE CAKE IS MY FAVOURITE FOOD."

Annas Saidi

Rachel's All-in-one Chocolate Cake

Rachel (Ella, Henry and Lucas Rowell)

MAKES ONE 8IN (20CM) CAKE

A quick and easy way to make a yummy chocolate cake, one of my favourite recipes and the kids love it! It's always a winner for birthday cakes and special treats. I usually crumble a Cadbury's Flake over the top to decorate.

CAKE:
8OZ (225G) SELF-RAISING FLOUR, SIEVED
8OZ (225G) CASTER SUGAR
8OZ (225G) BUTTER, SOFTENED
2OZ (50G) COCOA POWDER, SIEVED
4 MEDIUM EGGS, LIGHTLY BEATEN
2 TABLESPOONS MILK

BUTTERCREAM ICING:
8OZ (225G) BUTTER, SOFTENED
1LB (450G) ICING SUGAR, SIEVED
2OZ (50G) COCOA POWDER, SIEVED
1-2 TABLESPOONS HOT WATER

Preheat the oven to 150°C/300°F/Gas Mark 2 (fan-assisted). Grease and line a deep 8 inch/20cm cake tin. Place all the cake ingredients in one large mixing bowl and whisk by hand or with an electric mixer until combined. Spoon into the tin and bake in the centre of the oven for approximately 1 hour, or until a skewer inserted in the centre comes out clean and the top of the cake is springy to the touch. Leave to cool thoroughly (otherwise it will crumble) then slice in half horizontally. Whisk all the buttercream icing ingredients together and spread half the icing over the bottom layer. Sandwich the two halves together, top with the rest of the icing and decorate.

"THE BEST MEAL I'VE EVER EATEN IS CHOCLATE CAKE AT MY GRANDMA'S HOUSE."

Oliver D'Souza.

Strawberry Kiwi Tart

Noelle (mum to Adlane Maouche)

MAKES ONE 25CM TART (SERVES 6-8)

Strawberry tarts are very popular in France. In this recipe, whole or sliced strawberries and kiwis are arranged on a layer of crème mousseline (enriched pastry cream) in a baked sweet pastry shell, but you can use any fruit, for example apples or even lemons. When I was little my mum used to make it with whatever fruit was picked from the garden. I remember trying to finish my dinner quickly every night so I could get my fruit tart for pudding. I make it most weekends, and often make individual tarts instead of one large one. It's perfect for parties as the pastry case and the crème mousseline can be made the day before and the tart assembled a few hours before serving.

SWEET PASTRY:
250G PLAIN FLOUR
125G COLD UNSALTED BUTTER
1 EGG, SEPARATED
2 TABLESPOONS ICING SUGAR
1 PINCH SALT

CRÈME MOUSSELINE:
4 LEVEL TABLESPOONS CORN-
FLOUR
1/2L WHOLE MILK
2 EGG YOLKS
4 TABLESPOONS CASTER
SUGAR
50G BUTTER, CUT INTO
   SMALL PIECES
70ML CRÈME FRAICHE
80ML DOUBLE CREAM,
   WHIPPED UNTIL THICK
   (BUT NOT STIFF)

FRUIT TOPPING:
PUNNET OF FRESH STRAWBER
   RIES, WASHED, HULLED
   AND SLICED
1 KIWI, PEELED AND SLICED
2 TABLESPOONS STRAWBERRY
   OR APRICOT JAM
4 TABLESPOONS WATER

To make the pastry, mix the flour, sugar and salt together in a large bowl. Cut in the cold butter with a knife until the mixture is blended together and the bits of butter are the size of peas then rub in the butter gently with your fingertips until the mixture resembles fine crumbs (alternatively pulse in a food processor). Add the egg yolk (and a little egg white if more moisture is needed) and bring the mixture together into a dough. Form into a ball, place in a freezer bag and rest in the fridge for an hour. Remove the chilled dough from the fridge, and allow to come to room temperature.

Lightly grease a 25cm/11in loose-bottomed tart tin. Roll the pastry out on a lightly floured surface to a thickness of 5mm, roll it gently around the rolling pin and transfer it to the tin. Press it firmly against the sides and bottom, trim off any excess then cover and rest in the fridge for 30 minutes before blind-baking. Preheat the oven to 180°C/350°F/Gas Mark 4 and put a baking tray in the oven. Remove pastry from fridge, prick all over with a fork and line with baking parchment and baking beans. Place on the heated baking tray and bake for 15 minutes. Remove the baking parchment and bake for a further 15 minutes until lightly coloured. Remove from oven and allow to cool completely.

To make the crème mousseline, mix the cornflour with the milk then whisk in the egg yolks and sugar. Place in a saucepan and bring to the boil, then turn the heat down and stir continuously until the mixture has thickened (around 3 minutes). Remove from heat, whisk in the butter and leave to cool. Mix the crème fraiche and whipped double cream together. When the pastry cream is completely cool, gently incorporate the whipped cream.

To make the glaze, heat the jam and the water together until boiling and leave to cool. To assemble the tart, spread the crème mousseline on the tart base, then decorate with the fruit. Brush the glaze over the top. To prevent the delicate crust from breaking, leave in the tin while assembling the tart. Unmould just before serving, or cut into slices in the tin.

Brigadeiro (Brazilian Chocolate Truffles)

The Lieb Lerede family (Louise and Sophie)

MAKES APPROXIMATELY 25
BUT DEPENDS HOW BIG YOU ROLL THEM!

Brigadeiro is a typical Brazilian sweet, which is served at every Brazilian birthday party. Most adults come to children's birthday parties just for a chance to eat them!

1 CAN SWEETENED CONDENSED MILK
1 TABLESPOON BUTTER
2 TABLESPOONS COCOA
CHOCOLATE SPRINKLES, TO DECORATE
SMALL PAPER CASES (MINI MUFFIN
    CASES ARE FINE)

the pascual vallati family also thinks this is perfect for children's parties!

Put the condensed milk, butter and cocoa in a non-stick or heavy-bottomed pan and mix them all together. Let the mixture cook over a low heat for about 12 minutes, stirring constantly until the mixture loosens from the bottom of the pan and is thick like cream. (It's important that you don't stop stirring as it has a tendency to stick to the pan sides and burn!). Put the mixture on a greased plate and allow to cool down completely. Roll mixture into small balls, using about a teaspoon at a time. (This is easier if you grease your hands with butter beforehand and wash your hands once in a while). Put the sprinkles in a bowl and roll the small balls in them. Place in small paper cases and then on a serving plate.

Agnes' Pavlova

Agnes Howard-Jones

SERVES 6

I like pavlova because it is very yummy and simple to make. And you can put whatever you want on it. I prefer using strawberries and blueberries. Never use mango or raspberries because they will make the meringue soggy! You can make a chocolate meringue by adding a tablespoon of cocoa powder at the same time as the sugar.

FOR THE MERINGUE:
4 EGG WHITES
PINCH OF SALT
200G CASTER SUGAR
1 TEASPOON CORNFLOUR
1 TEASPOON VANILLA ESSENCE
1 TEASPOON LEMON JUICE

FOR THE TOPPING:
42ML CARTON DOUBLE CREAM
150G LOW FAT NATURAL
    YOGURT
A MIXTURE OF ABOUT 500G
    OF YOUR FAVOURITE FRESH
    FRUITS

Preheat the oven to 140°C/275°F/Gas Mark 1. Prepare a baking sheet by covering it with a piece of baking parchment. Put the egg whites into a large, very clean, dry mixing bowl and place the bowl on a damp cloth to stop it slipping. Add the salt and, using an electric mixer, whisk until stiff. Add the sugar gradually, whisking until very stiff. Stir in the cornflour, vanilla essence and lemon juice. Spoon onto the baking sheet and shape into a circle, about 3cm deep. Bake for around 1 hour, until pale brown and hard to the touch. Remove from the oven and leave to cool. Peel the paper off when completely cool.

Put the cream into a bowl and whisk until thick. Add the yoghurt and fold it into the cream with a spoon. Spread the cream and yoghurt over the cold meringue and arrange the fruit over the top of the cream.

Thank yous

This is a book about food, but first and foremost it is a book about community. A sense of community can't just be magicked up out of thin-air by think tanks or policy units (much to the chagrin of vote-hungry politicians). Communities – particularly where there is great diversity (of age and ability; values and opinions; backgrounds and cultures) – need a shared purpose or interest to bring them together. When we kicked off our small cookbook project, almost a year ago, to raise funds for a new school library, we were expecting the usual lethargy from a school community wearied from too many demands on their wallet and time. How wrong we were. Over 150 recipes were submitted by the deadline, with almost as many accompanying photos. Parents literally chased us down the road to tell their stories and share, with pride, their food memories. And local businesses bent over backwards to help us, too. Which just goes to show that there are few subjects with as much universal appeal as food! We feel truly proud that our small community in South West London has come together to produce a harvest of so many interesting stories. Thank you to everyone who made it happen…

The parents

A big thank you to Sally Le Marquand and Lucy Uden, the co-chairs of FOBG (the Friends of Bishop Gilpin, aka the PTA), who patiently supported this project throughout and took a leap of faith in agreeing to fund the not inconsiderable cost of printing the book. If (when!) they do actually see a return on their investment, it will be down to the hard work of all the parents who gave up their time to this project for free (many of whom spent hours burning the midnight oil once they had finished running after their children and/or their day job). Enormous thanks to Basia Paczesna-Vercueil, our brilliant graphic designer and mum of four, for the many months spent tweaking, cropping and juggling – how blessed we are to have had you on the team! Thanks also to our three amazing professional photographers – Deborah Albert, Sampson Lloyd and Francesca McKenna – and our talented amateur, Tom Hopkinson; printing guru Paul Regan, who helped get the project off the ground and – with the help of his company F.E. Burman – made our photography competition possible; Jo McIntosh, our treasurer; Wendy Drummer, who hunted down a ton of email addresses; caterer extraordinaire Elaine Harper-Jones, who baked the cakes that we gave away in the playground as an incentive to get families to pledge recipes; and Charlotte Van Der Goltz, who opened up her beautiful home for the 'Bonfire Night' photo shoot. Plus all the parents who managed to cook the dishes needed for (and deliver them intact to!) the seven photo shoot locations: Cat Brown (Swedish Cinnamon Buns); Christobel Boydell (Granny's Bullets); Claire Coppin (Butternut Squash and Feta Salad); Fiona Cunningham (Greek Roast Lamb, Spanakopita Real Greek Salad, Authentic Greek Tsatsiki); Wendy Drummer (Sausagemeat Pie); Mrs Gill (Toffee Apple Flapjacks); Sarah Gower (Carrot Cake); Laura Greenaway (Spicy Pumpkin Soup); Elaine Harper-Jones (Grandma's Bonfire Night Treacle Tart, Elaine's Cupcakes, All-In-One Victoria Sandwich, Strawberry Kiwi Tart); Julie Haynes (The Ultimate Chilli); Dorthe Hermansen (Vanilla Sugar Cookies, Danish Peppernuts, Danish Honey Biscuits, Christmas Klejner, Coconut Balls); Tristan Hopkinson (Toffee Apples, Severed Fingers, Halloween Cupcakes); Jane Long (Chocolate Fudge Cake); Kerstin Ludwig (Swabian Lentil Stew, Baked Lollipops); Ana Navas (Spanish Lentil Soup with Chorizo); Jane Park (Rocky Road); Marion Rea (Go Faster Banana Bread, Chocolate Brownies, Lamingtons); The Reed Family (Lemon and Raspberry Cakes); Tina Roux (German Cheesecake); Zeinegul Salimova (Baursaks); Simone Tromans (Cornish Buttermilk Scones); Charlotta Trygg Bolton (Swedish Banana Cake); Ambreen Vellani (Lamb Biryani); Gill Williams (Rutland Gingerbread); Vicky Williams-Ellis (Bacon Pasties) and the obento mums: Kyoko Boheringer, Mayumi Ishiguro, Hiroko McIsaac, Satomi Mearashi and Miki Miyasaka. Special thanks to: Dorthe Hermansen, who managed to convince the Danish mums that Christmas had come early; Hiroko McIsaac, who coordinated the marathon obento making session; Fiona Cunningham – a one-woman wonder – who cooked up a whole 'Greek Easter' feast by herself; and Elaine Harper-Jones, Marion Rea and Kerstin Ludwig (all of whom never, ever said no to our multiple baking requests, even though we probably nearly tipped them over the edge on several occasions).

Thanks also to all the families who cooked their dishes at home and took photos, many of which have ended up in the book.

Last, but not least, thank you to the intrepid cookbook team, who provided creative flair (Ruth Mair Howard-Jones), some playground muscle (Emma Helbert and Jane Long), a steady pair of hands (Marion Rea), a calming voice (Tristan Hopkinson and Sally Le Marquand), a careful eye (Susannah Hamilton and Kate Oppenheim), sage advice (Katie Preston and Vicky Williams-Ellis) a sturdy shoulder (Christobel Boydell) or just someone to rock up to a shoot and eat the food (Danielle Phillips!).

The staff

The project would never have gone ahead without the support of the staff, in particular Mr Ball, our Headteacher, who helped us involve the children during assembly and let us invade the staff room for our 'Afternoon Tea' photo shoot; the teachers who organised drawings and quotes for us from the children; and Mrs Wardell and Mrs Michel, who patiently put up with all the cake tins, vintage china, posters, photographs, handwritten recipes and other random items that periodically cluttered up their office in the name of the project.

Everyone else!

Thank you to everyone in the community who helped us in our hours of need! Photographer Kitty Gallannaugh took the fabulous photos for the 'Greek Easter' shoot; two gallant organisations used their office printers to print our colour proof copies at very short notice – thankyou Martin from local printing firm Purbrooks for helping out small fry like us, and Alison from Hamptons Wimbledon Village for charming your IT department and hand-delivering our print-out personally. Maplins Wimbledon gave us a digital camera (an incentive for our families to take photographs of their recipes); the wonderful art supplies shop and Wimbledon institution Fielders furnished us with materials for our photography competition; florist Brian Kirkby provided us with the flowers for our Easter table and Wimbledon Wine Cellar for the Greek wines (authenticity in such matters being important!). Charlie Williams-Ellis, our 11 year old IT consultant, set us up with a Facebook page early on in the project when we needed to drum up enthusiasm. Five lovely graphic designers (Kimberly Geswein, Antoniu@fuzzimo.com, Denise Bentulan@Douxiegirl.com, Robert Norgren@robertnorgren.com and Ray Larabie@TypodermicFonts.com) waived their fee for use of fonts and images. And we would have been utterly lost without the wonderful and talented freelance graphic designer Alessandra Ferrari Ellis, who stepped in to help us meet our print deadline at the eleventh hour. Thank you Aless, for giving up your time so generously. You did a brilliant job!

Final thanks to our families, who may never want to pick up a cookbook again, especially Baz, Evie, Grace; and Big Derik, Sofia, Ania, Little Derik and the amazingly patient and beautiful princess, Olivia.

Alessandra Ferrari-Ellis (www.alessandraellis.com)
Basia Pacześna-Vercueil (www.whatbasiamade.com)
Brian Kirkby Flowers (www.briankirkbyflowers.co.uk)
Deborah Albert (www.deborahalbert.co.uk)
Elaine Harper-Jones (www.facebook.com/cakesinwimbledon)
F.E. Burman (www.feburman.co.uk)
Fielders (www.fielders.co.uk)
Francesca McKenna (www.akilipix.com)
Hamptons International (www.hamptons.co.uk)
Kitty Gallanaugh (www.kittygallannaugh.com)
Maplins (www.maplin.co.uk)
Purbrooks (www.purbrooks.co.uk)
Sampson Lloyd (www.sampsonlloyd.com)
Wimbledon Wine Cellar (www.wimbledonwinecellar.com)

Index

Apples

Apple Sharlotka 23 v
Apple, Pear and Vanilla
  Compote 25 v
Apples with Cinnamon 23 v
Dutch Apple Pie (Hollandse
  Appeltaart) 24 v
Sticky Maple-Apple Traybake 46 v
Toffee Apple Flapjacks 20 v
Toffee Apples 47 v

Beef

Beef Stroganoff 80
Bulgogl (Korean Barbecue) 152
Chupe (Peruvian Soup) 80
Colombian Empanadas 146
Gao's Dumplings 94
Mr Rob's Steak and Chips 97
The Ultimate Chilli 52

Biscuits

Danish Honey Biscuits 56 v
Danish Peppernuts 58 v
Easter Biscuits 113 v
Gingerbread Men 141 v
Great Aunt Elsie's Honey
  Jumbles 60 v
South African Rusks 14 v
Vanilla Sugar Cookies (Sofus
  Vanilladreams) 56 v
Yummy Oat Biscuits 130 v

Blackberries

Wimbledon Common Clafoutis 25 v

Blueberries

Agnes' Pavlova 155 v
Finnish Blueberry Dessert 125 v
Nicholas' Breakfast Smoothie 15 v

Bread

Chapati (Roti) 36 v
Flatbread 36 v
Guinness Brown Bread 84 v
Preston-Style Pizza 120 v
Wheaten Bread (Wholemeal Soda
Bread) 83 v

Cakes, Bakes and Batters

After-School Syrup Cake 132 v
All-in-one Victoria Sandwich 100 v
American Chocolate Chip
  Cookies 132 v

Apple Sharlotka 23 v
Baked Lollipops 89 v
Canadian Pancakes 12 v
Hummingbird Bakery Carrot
  Cake 102 v
Cheeseburger Cakes 90 v
Chocolate Brownies 90 v
Christmas Klejner 58 v
Dutch Pancakes 93 v
Elaine's Cupcakes 88 v
Fruit Bar 131 v
German Buttermilk Waffles 15 v
Go-Faster Banana Bread 21 v
Halloween Cupcakes 44 v
Lamingtons 91 v
Lemon and Raspberry Cakes 103 v
Niamh's Moist Chocolate
  Loaf Cake 153 v
Nick Long's Chocolate
  Fudge Cake 101 v
Rachel's All-In-One Chocolate
  Cake 153 v
Rocky Road 89 v
Rutland Gingerbread 53 v
South African Rusks 14 v
Sticky Maple-Apple Traybake 46 v
Swedish Banana Cake 21 v
Swedish Cinnamon Buns 18 v
Toffee Apple Flapjacks 20 v
Wholemeal Mini Pancakes 11 v
Wimbledon Cake 135 v

Chicken

Caramel Chicken 27
Cheat's Chicken Korma 117
Chicken and Lentil Soup 77
Chicken Curry 34
Coronation Chicken 134
Creamy Mustard and Tarragon
  Chicken 118
Green Chilli Chicken 31
Minimal Washing-up Chicken
  Dinner 116
Oma's Chicken Soup 76
Quesedillas 140
Tanya's Chicken Goujons 140
Thai Green Chicken Curry 142

Chocolate

American Chocolate Chip
  Cookies 132 v
Chocolate Brownies 90 v
Deer's Back 41
Edd's Toblerone Pudding 124 v

Lamingtons 91 v
Niamh's Moist Chocolate Loaf
  Cake 153 v
Nick Long's Chocolate Fudge
  Cake 101 v
Rachel's All-In-One Chocolate
  Cake 153 v
Robin's Chocolate Apricots 141 v
Rocky Road 89 v
Swedish Gino (White Chocolate
  & Fruit Gratin) 125 v
White Chocolate and Raspberry
  Brioche Pudding 124 v

Drinks

Hot Chocolate with Cardamom 19 v
Nicholas' Breakfast Smoothie 13 v
Vin Chaud 65 v

Duck

Iranian Duck, Walnut and Pomegranate Stew (Khoresht Fesenjän) 28

Eggs

Child-Friendly Omelette 72 v
Eggy Bread 11 v
Pastry-less Quiche Lorraine 70 v
Yummy 'Never-Fail' Cheese
  Soufflé 64 v

Fish

Bengali Fish Curry 34
Catalan Paella 144
Easy Fish Pie 127
Fried Prawns with Wasabi
  Mayonnaise 127
Grandma's Christmas Eve Fish
  Pie 65
Mr Ball's Sea Bass with a Lemon
  and Butter Sauce 96
Pressed Sushi (Oshi-sushi) 129
Salt Fish and Ackee 128
Sweet Potato and Smoked
  Mackerel Jackets 128
Tuna Sashimi 97

Lamb

Irish Stew 83
Lamb Baked in the Oven
  (Arni Sto Fourno) 109
Lamb Biryani 30
Lamb Karahi 32
Rice and Broad Beans with Lamb 148
Shaslik 151

Lentils

Chicken and Lentil Soup 77
Spanish Lentil Soup with Chorizo 80
Ballymaloe Spicy Lentil Burgers 71
Sri Lankan Lentil Curry
with Spinach 72 v
Swabian Lentil Stew with Frankfurters
(Linsen mit Saitenwürstchen) 74

Muesli & Porridge

Apple & Cinammon Porridge 11 v
Apple Muesli 11 v

Pasta

Ben's Tuna Pasta 122
Jamie Oliver's Cauliflower
Macaroni 70 v
Pasta Iris 122 v

Pastry

Bacon Pasties 50
Dutch Apple Pie (Hollandse
Appeltaart) 24 v
Grandma's Bonfire Night Treacle
Tart 53 v
Granny's Bullets (Mince Pies) 66 v
Quick Tomato Tart 119 v
Sausagemeat Pie 20
Spanakopita (Spinach and Feta
Pie) 110 v
Strawberry Kiwi Tart 154 v

Pears

Apple, Pear and Vanilla
Compote 25 v

Pork

Good Old Bacon Butty 133
Scottish Stovies 82

Puddings

Agnes's Pavlova 155 v
Baursaks (Mini Doughnuts) 105 v
Chocolate Brownies 90 v
Deer's Back 41 v
Easy Lime Cheesecake 124
Edd's Toblerone Pudding 124 v
Finnish Blueberry Dessert 125 v
Frangelico Tiramisu 40 v
German Cheesecake 103 v

Grandma's Bonfire Night Treacle
Tart 53 v
Graveyard Jellies 44
Lemon Surprise Pudding 85 v
Maggie's Christmas Pudding 62 v
Mrs Wardell's Black Forest Cake 42 v
Passion Fruit Mousse (Mousse
de Maracuj) 96 v
Quick Strawberry Ice Cream 135 v
Swedish Gino (White Chocolate
& Fruit Gratin) 125 v
White Chocolate and Raspberry
Brioche Pudding 124
Wimbledon Common Clafoutis 25 v

Raspberries

Lemon and Raspberry Cakes 103 v
White Chocolate and Raspberry
Brioche Pudding 124 v

Salads

Alexander's English Breakfast
Salad 15 v
Butternut and Feta Salad 150 v
Real Greek Salad 111 v

Sauces

Authentic Greek Tsatsiki 111 v
Guacamole 147 v
Persian Yoghurt and Cucumber
(Maast-o-Khiar) 39 v
Raisin Sauce for Ham 67 v
Raita 39 v

Sides

Braised Spiced Red Cabbage 84 v
Chestnut Stuffing 67 v
Mandy's Magnificent Mielie
Bake 151 v
Perfect Basmati Rice 38 v
Persian Rice (Polow) 38 v
Pickled Cucumber 85 v
Sage and Onion Stuffing 73 v
Spätzle (Swabian Noodles) 74 v
Vegetable Pilau Rice (Pulao) 38 v
Yellow Rice 38 v

Soup

Chicken and Lentil Soup 77
Chupe (Peruvian Soup) 80

Leek & Potato Soup 77 v
Oma's Chicken Soup 76
Spanish Lentil Soup with Chorizo 80
Spicy Pumpkin Soup 50 v
Ukrainian Borsch 78

Strawberries

Agnes's Pavlova 155 v
Quick Strawberry Ice Cream 135 v
Strawberry Kiwi Tart 154 v

Sweet Potatoes

Moosewood West African Groundnut
Stew 73 v
Sweet Potato and Smoked Mackerel
Jackets 128

Sweets (Candy)

Brigadeiro (Brazilian Chocolate
Truffles) 155 v
Coconut Balls 59 v
Crunchy Toffee 47 v
Peppermint Bark 59 v
Scottish Tablet 61 v
Toffee Apples 47 v

Veal

Veal in Cream and Mushroom Sauce
(Geschnetzeltes) 27

v denotes recipes without meat or fish
NB Some processed ingredients may be derived from animals, so please check packet)

photo credits:

Photographs taken by our families appear on the following pages:
12, 14, 22, 25, 27, 28, 29, 31, 36, 37, 39, 46, 51, 61, 62, 63, 72, 78, 82, 83, 85, 93, 95, 96, 112, 119, 120, 121, 122, 127, 129, 132, 135, 143, 145, 149, 150, 152, 153, 157, 158

Photographs taken by our professional photographers, and a few roving amateurs, appear on the following pages:

Deborah Albert : 16, 18, 19, 20, 21, 35, 68-69, 86, 87, 88, 90, 91, 142, 156
Kitty Gallanaugh: 106, 107, 108, 109, 110 and the front cover
Sampson Lloyd: 26, 43, 48, 49, 50, 52, 53, 55, 56, 57, 60, 74, 75, 81, 97, 98, 99, 100, 101, 102, 103, 104, 105, 114, 122, 123, 133, 135, 152
Francesca McKenna: 10, 16, 33, 35, 59, 60, 71, 114, 128, 139, 140, 141

Mel Barrett: 30, 154
Christobel Boydell: 2
Tom Hopkinson: 2-3, 45, 126, 134, 135
Basia Pacześna-Vercueil: 112-113, 114, 134, 142, 160